MW00973524

PATTERNS AND PRAYERS

FOR

CHRISTIAN WORSHIP

A guidebook for worship leaders

Ripon Upon of Great Britain

OXFORD UNIVERSITY PRESS

PATTERNS AND PRAYERS
FOR
CHRISTIAN WORSHIP

A guidebook for worship leaders

Baptist Union of Great Britain

OXFORD UNIVERSITY PRESS

Oxford University Press, Walton Street, Oxford OX2 6DP

Oxford New York
Athens Auckland Bangkok Bombay
Calcutta Cape Town Dar es Salaam Delhi
Florence Hong Kong Istanbul Karachi
Kuala Lumpur Madras Madrid Melbourne
Mexico City Nairobi Paris Singapore
Taipei Tokyo Toronto
and associated companies in
Berlin Ibadan

Oxford is a trade mark of Oxford University Press

British Library Cataloguing in Publication Data
Data available

ISBN 0-19-144081-7

Printed in Great Britain
on acid-free paper

Contents

Preface

Baptists have their roots deep within the Free Church tradition. Therefore the freedom of the Holy Spirit is a significant factor in their worship, and they do not have a fixed liturgy or approved prayer-book. This does not mean that worship has no shape or basic content, or that preparation and forms are despised. Over the past sixty years a number of books have been published by the Baptist Union, providing practical guidance in the leading of worship and prayer material suitable for a variety of special occasions as well as Sunday worship.

The most recent of these guides have been *Orders and Prayers for Church Worship: a manual for ministers* compiled by E. A. Payne and S. F. Winward and first published in 1960, and *Praise God: a collection of resource material for Christian Worship*, by Alec Gilmore, Edward Smalley, and Michael Walker, first published in 1980.

Recent years have brought many changes in the approach to worship and in its language. There is now a wide variety of practice, from liturgical formality to charismatic exuberance, from reformed traditionalism to ecumenical experiment. In such a context and in response to widespread demand it has been judged that a new guide for leaders of worship is needed. This book is the result.

In January 1988 the General Purposes and Finance Committee of the Baptist Union of Great Britain commissioned the following people to work on the production of a new worship manual:

> the Revds Bernard Green, MA, BD (chairman), Christopher Ellis, MA, MPhil., Rachel Harrison, MA, MTh., Stuart Jenkins, BA, Michael Nicholls, BD, MTh., and Tony Turner, BA.

In the course of the work the group consulted widely with representatives of the Baptist Ministers' Fellowship (who also provided the results of their research among a group of young ministers), the Federation of Lay Ministries, and some churches strongly influenced by the Renewal Movement. When drafts of various sections of the book were sufficiently developed, they were field-tested by a cross-section of Baptist ministers and we are grateful for their insights and criticisms. The section on Ministry was shared with Baptist College Principals and the General Superintendents of the Baptist Union. Their incisive comments were most valuable.

In particular we are grateful to Dr John Biggs, MA, CChem., FRSC, a lecturer at the University of Hull and a former President of the Baptist Union, for his assessment and advice as our literary consultant. Similarly we thank the Revd Dr Derek Tidball, BA, BD, minister of Mutley Baptist Church, Plymouth, and President of the Baptist Union (1990–1991), who has given considerable advice as a biblical consultant. Mrs Faith Bowers, BA, MPhil., has undertaken an immense amount of word-processing and detailed sub-editing to assist me in preparing the final manuscript for the publishers. We owe her a big debt of thanks, as we do to my secretary, Miss Dora Smith, who has answered more telephone calls, copied more documents, arranged more meetings, and typed more letters than I dare assess.

This book could not have been published without the help of all these people. We warmly acknowledge their services. Responsibility for the final product rests entirely on the editorial group.

Our aim has been to provide a book, not only for ministers, but also for all who prepare and lead worship. We have tried to provide patterns of worship, resource material, and guide-lines for those whose worship is liturgical, traditional, or informal and spontaneous. The units of material are interchangeable and we hope that the book will prompt people to develop their own patterns rather than look to these pages for settled and fixed forms.

We have written primarily for Baptists, but not exclusively so. We hope that our efforts will prove useful to Christians of all persuasions in Britain and overseas. In particular we trust that in the contemporary ecumenical scene this book will be seen as a worthy expression of Baptist identity, which will make a useful contribution to the process of learning from one another.

Finally, we have endeavoured to be inclusive in language. We have also attempted to combine material from the rich heritage of Christian liturgy and prayer with contemporary styles and words, without losing the reverence and dignity which are proper to the worship of almighty God. To him be the glory!

BERNARD GREEN

July 1990

CHRISTIAN WORSHIP

How we understand it

While many Baptists would expect the one leading their worship to use extempore prayer, there is still a large place within Baptist worship both for written prayer and for the use of formal orders of worship. A new book is now offered to inspire and enrich the Church's worship, providing practical guidance in the leading of worship and prayer material suitable for a variety of occasions.

FLEXIBLE PATTERNS

We often speak of 'orders of service'. When a church has a visiting speaker, an order of service is sent with the warm invitation to alter it. Change rarely occurs. In contrast, the worship of many congregations is deliberately spontaneous and allows free participation. Experience shows that it is wrong to assume that the Spirit is necessarily more manifest in a free form of worship than in a structured form.

It is hoped that the new worship book will have an educative role within the Baptist community, encouraging people to enrich their worship, whatever their tradition, by the use of new material, prayers from other parts of the Christian Church, and a fresh reflection on distinctive Baptist emphases. It will link Baptists with the world Church, and enrich each local church and those who lead its regular worship. The book presents Spirit-inspired patterns to meet every local need.

CLEAR DEFINITION

To worship is to acknowledge God's worth in acts of praise as well as in daily life. Within the whole of life there will be acts of worship which ought to be, in Karl Barth's words, 'the most momentous, the most urgent, the most glorious action' that can ever take place. Such worship is the focus of the relationship between God and people. God makes himself known to us and we respond. We listen as God speaks to us in Scripture, as the Word is preached, and as God's gift of redemption is visualized in the sacraments. The Word is made audible and visible. We respond to God's love with our praises, our prayers, and the offering of our whole selves. When we gather for worship we desire to discern God's will so that we may carry it out in daily life. We must discover how contemporary acts of Baptist worship can become those in which the mind, heart, and imagination are fully engaged with God. Worship is a dialogue in which God and his people speak with one another.

RICH VARIETY

It is anticipated that in the coming years Christians of various church traditions will become more aware of each others' patterns of worship. Baptists have always enjoyed a variety of patterns of worship. Some express freedom through participatory and open worship; others emphasize order through a Reformed structure of service.

In the seventeenth and eighteenth centuries there were animated debates over forms of worship. In the ferment of the nineteenth century preaching was exalted above everything else. Acts of praise became the preliminaries and the celebration of the sacraments the addendum to the main course of the feast.

In the early years of the twentieth century morning services were largely attended by members and offered opportunities for a teaching ministry both to children and adults. Evening services had a much stronger evangelistic emphasis.

Since the nineteen-fifties much of this has changed. Mornings have brought family services, while evening congregations have become smaller. The atmosphere is usually more informal; many translations of scripture are used; the language and style of prayer have changed; members of the congregation often participate. To those who appreciate novelty all this is welcome. To others it is disturbing. To some churches have come freshness and vitality; to others restlessness and dissension.

DIFFERENT INFLUENCES

Within the latter years of the twentieth century the Lord's Supper has generally become an integral part of the service. Responsive participation by the congregation in wide-ranging liturgy has become a prominent feature. The liturgical movement has had widespread influence on Baptist churches through ecumenical contact. During the nineteen-sixties there was a crisis of confidence in the bible and in preaching, together with an increased emphasis on family church. At the same time Roman Catholics have engaged more willingly with Protestants.

This has opened up for increasing numbers of Baptists an awareness of the mystical and contemplative traditions of the Church. In more recent years the charismatic movement has laid renewed emphasis upon the gifting of the Holy Spirit. There has been an overwhelming temptation to shape liturgy to fit consumer needs. The fact that at the present time the charismatic and ecumenical movements have influenced many Baptist churches has led to wide diversity of practice and preference. Indeed, it is true to say that Baptists historically represent an evangelical commitment to Word and sacrament, a catholic emphasis on tradition and fellowship, and a charismatic stress on gifting and participation. To that must be added the need for worship to be culturally relevant, since increased numbers of new adult converts have no previous experience of Sunday school or church.

THEOLOGICAL PRINCIPLES

Within this context certain theological principles need to be reflected in Baptist practice.

Biblical basis

Baptist worship has always centred on the Word of God and the patterns that are found in it. Any approach to worship must be set in the context of Jesus' desire for true worship, spelt out in John 4: 24. Here the Father desires those who will worship to do so in the light of Jesus the Truth, who has come in life, death, and resurrection, and the consequent giving of the Spirit. As the early Church developed its worship, its origins were threefold—scriptural in the synagogue background of Judaism, sacramental in the Upper Room practice, and pentecostal in the coming of the Spirit at Pentecost.

It is sad that in many ways through the centuries these traditions have been represented almost exclusively by Protestantism, Catholicism, and Pentecostalism respectively. The Bible urges us to bring them together. Equally, when one examines the features of New Testament worship, one could list teaching, singing, communion, participation, offering, praise, prayer, baptism. If one examines the practice in the church of Jerusalem in Acts 2, Antioch in Acts 13, and Corinth in 1 Corinthians 14, there is an infinite variety.

Gathered community

All this indicates that, just as the Spirit gave gifts to believers in the name of the Risen Christ to bring glory to him and to edify his body ready for ministry in the world, so all our worship needs to glorify God and build up his people for ministry.

For that to happen to the whole of God's people there needs to be a rich, united, and mature diversity in worship that is comprehensive, affirming that Christ has died, has risen, has been exalted, and is coming again. This confession affects the whole of life. It is worship offered by all God's gifted, gathered people.

In order to express this community of believers gathered around Christ, churches which use chairs instead of pews might profitably arrange them in a circle.

Visible expression

Since the nineteen-sixties there has been a perceptible shift in Baptist concepts of Baptism and the Lord's Supper. Our denomination has been delivered from seeing these ordinances as symbolic actions, personal confessions of faith, or times of individual praise. Baptism has become far more an act of obedience in which God meets with men and women as they demonstrate the reality of their repentance and identify with Christ in membership of his body, participation in his Supper, and the life of his Spirit. The Lord's Supper has become a much more central act of worship in which there is a looking back to the Cross, forward to the Coming, upward to the Risen Christ, inward for personal salvation, and outward for the corporate dimension of fellowship.

This rich sacramental life has implications for the practice of worship. For instance, there are those who believe that Baptism ought to be linked to the Lord's Supper and membership, but this belief is not always put into practice because there may be uncommitted people present at the Lord's Table. This raises the question of whether worship is for the believing community or for others. There are similar questions concerning the presence of children at the Lord's Supper and who should participate in the event.

Spirit led

Contemporary Baptist practice has inevitably been influenced by large numbers from other denominations who now worship in local Baptist churches. Much greater attention is paid to the Christian festivals within the calendar year. Such occasions demand special material which can enhance their importance. Equally, contemporary emphasis on family worship and instruction raises the question of what is appropriate for the church family when children are present. Renewed emphasis upon open or free worship indicates the need for meaningful structures, so that freedom and flexibility can operate within guidelines of order and unity.

All this means that any manual for worship-leaders must contain comprehensive material which enables special services to be conducted with dignity, relevance, and practicality. It should also enable imaginative plans to be drawn up to enrich and fertilize the minds of those whom the Spirit uses to guide our services so that all our practices relate to the principles of Scripture, the historical tradition of the Church, and the contemporary needs of believers as they live in the world.

COMPETENT GUIDANCE

Evangelical worship can lose its sense of direction. The idea of movement implicit in some of the traditional orders of service needs to be retained. God has indeed poured out his Spirit upon his people in a new way. Many pastors have abdicated their traditional role of leading worship and handed it over to the church's musicians. Yet there is a clear difference between leading songs and leading worship. To lead a congregation in worship is to be entrusted with one of the most important tasks of the church. Those who lead acts of worship in which many participate require:

- the training and development of gifts
- the ability to guide the service in order to avoid cross-currents of emotion and ambition
- structures to include praise, proclamation, and prayer
- direction to move the people on sensitively and expectantly
- strength to provide confidence and security.

It is one thing to express personal devotion, but quite another to lead God's people in worship. We hope this book will be used to guide and inspire those who are called to such an important task.

Planning Worship

The programme of a Sunday service can be put on paper as an 'Order of Service', a list of headings that describes the various items in sequence: Call to Worship, Hymn, Prayer, Reading, and so on. Orders of Service are very useful to those leading worship and to others taking part, but they may conceal the underlying pattern of the service. The heading 'Prayer' may occur several times, but at these points in the service it will not be the same prayer which is offered, because different things are happening as the service progresses. Also, an Order of Service, being a bare list of items to be said or sung, may distract attention from actions that take place, such as the offering being brought forward, or music being played, which are important parts of worship. Planning a service is obviously much more than making an Order of Service: we need to begin by developing a feel for the patterns of worship.

The meaning of 'pattern' can be derived from Paul's words about worship in 1 Corinthians 14: 40: 'But let all be done decently and in order'. The Greek word translated 'decently' is also the origin of the word 'scheme'. It conveys the idea of things co-ordinated to a common purpose and points to a pattern which has its own inner logic.

Earlier in the chapter Paul writes, 'For God is not a God of disorder but of peace' (verse 33), and in Genesis we are told that the Spirit of God moved upon the waters (Genesis 1: 2) bringing order out of chaos. This is more than a statement about how the world was begun: it is a claim that this is how the world always is, held in orderly existence by God's Spirit which pervades all things. Yet the Spirit is not a creator of stereotypes. It is the unexpected that occurs within the basic pattern that is stimulating and exciting. Though all roses are the same, no two are ever identical. The elusive quality we call beauty is seen in the variations that give liveliness and interest. Worship too should have an underlying order that is not a chain but an invitation to freedom.

Worship is at the centre of our relationship with God and our life together as the Body of Christ in the world. Although we have great freedom in the way we worship, we can point to certain elements which will always reappear, though not necessarily in the same form or even in any one service. These are the 'ingredients' of worship:

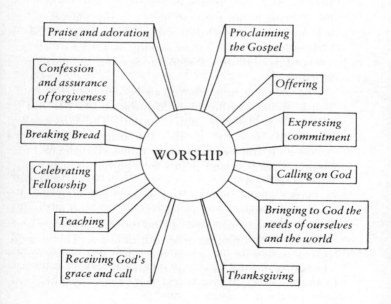

The diagram deliberately avoids arranging the ingredients according to one set pattern. Christians throughout history have used a variety of forms of worship and there is no single pattern which can claim supremacy. However, every act of worship does need a pattern, and this must take account of the nature of the various ingredients of worship.

We worship God because he is the Lord, and in **praise and adoration** we lift him up and glorify him as **our** Lord. In the many hymns and songs of adoration and in prayer we turn our attention away from ourselves and towards God, praising him for what he is and what he has done. Adoration is often poetic in style, since it needs to engage emotions as well as minds. References to 'psalms, hymns, and spiritual songs' (e.g. Ephesians 5: 19) show that the early Church followed and extended the Jews' belief in the priority of praise.

To give God his due praise is also to acknowledge our dependence on him. God is not at our beck and call, so worship will generally begin by **calling on God** so that by his gracious presence we may be caught up into the great movement of love into which he invites us. Realizing our dependence on God will also naturally and properly lead us into **thanksgiving** as we express our gratitude to God who is not merely good but good to us.

Confession acknowledges the gulf between God and us, between what we are and what God would have us to be. It is more than an apology or a recital of sins, and deals with our fears and shortcomings. This realism about what and who we are is essential to a true meeting with God. Confession can lead on to **bringing our needs** and failings before God in prayer, or it may be followed by the **assurance of forgiveness** as we remember that God does not count our sins against us.

In the reading of scripture and in preaching, the **Gospel is proclaimed**. This is **teaching** to strengthen the Church (1 Corinthians 14: 26), and also an encounter with God. As the sermon holds us in creative contact with God's Word, we **receive his grace and call**.

The Lord's Supper has always been central to Christian worship. The **breaking of bread** and sharing of wine also proclaim the Gospel, though with actions rather than words, and again we receive from God. But the Lord's Supper is a **celebration of friendship** too (1 Corinthians 11: 17–34), which renews our life in God and our oneness as the Body of Christ.

Offering relates to the whole of worship and not just to what we do with the money. We offer all that we bring in worship—our praise and prayers, money, bread and wine; our response is also an offering—of commitment, praise, giving, and service. The offering of gifts can perfectly well stand as part of opening worship, or may be preferred as part of our response to the ministry of the Word.

Prayer has a broad purpose in worship. As well as praise and confession we may also **express commitment** in prayer. This is likely to be part of our response to the Word. Prayer also provides the opportunity for us to **bring the needs of the world** before God. Such prayer should never become a mere list of wants, nor should it tell God what to do: he is neither ignorant nor in need of prompting. In prayer, in Christ's name, we lift up the world before God. To offer prayer for others is a privilege God has given us in Christ, a sharing in his ministry of love, and part of the priestly calling of the People of God.

It is helpful to divide worship into three stages: Approach to God, God's Word, and Our Response. The ingredients of worship are suited by their nature to one or more of these three sections:

Approach to God

The congregation takes its bearings on God—

> whose calling of us is remembered,
>
> and who is praised and adored;

and on itself—

> in confession,
>
> in expressing thanksgiving,
>
> and in the celebration of its fellowship.

Calling on God
Calling to worship
Adoration
Confession
Prayer for ourselves
Assurance of forgiveness
Thanksgiving
News and notices
Family awareness
Offering

God's Word

The Word is read and proclaimed in teaching and preaching. God is called on to interpret it to us, and the congregation and the world are brought into creative contact with the good news of Jesus Christ.

Reading
Prayer for illumination
Thanksgiving
Praise
Proclamation

Our Response

The congregation responds in thanksgiving and offering, in commitment and the ministry of prayer. At the table the gospel is remembered and received, the new relationship is celebrated and fellowship is renewed. The congregation departs to its life of service and witness.

Thanksgiving
Commitment
Offering
Prayer for ourselves
Prayer for the Church
Prayer for the world
The Lord's Supper
Praise
Blessing
Dismissal

The next stage is to construct an order of service, for example:

Call to worship	A summons or scripture sentences
Hymn	Invocation or adoration
Prayer	Praise, thanksgiving, and/or confession
Family talk	Celebrating all-age fellowship and introducing the theme of the readings
Hymn or Song	Thanksgiving or invocation of the Spirit
Readings	Old and New Testament
Sermon	Brings together the Word, the worshippers, and the world
Prayer	Initial response in praise, commitment, or seeking God's help
Hymn	Praise, restatement of gospel, or intercession
Offering	Gifts are presented and in prayer these and lives of service are offered
Prayer	Mainly for others but also for worshippers returning to life in the world
Hymn	Commitment or praise
Blessing	Dismissing one another in God's name

Other patterns of worship can be found later in the book. The three following examples of Sunday worship without communion indicate the variety possible.

First Pattern

Call to worship

Hymn of praise

Prayer of thanksgiving

Prayer of confession

Introduction to the theme—
  children and others go into groups

In groups, through readings and drama,
  discussion, sermon or craftwork,
  the theme is explored.

Groups reassemble for the offering of gifts

Hymn of response

Fellowship news, and notices

Prayers for others

The Lord's Prayer

Hymn of commitment

Benediction

Second Pattern

Approach to God and the Church's Praise
    Call to worship
    Hymn of praise
    Prayer of adoration and thanksgiving
    Prayer of confession
    Psalm
    Songs of worship

Faith in God
    Testimony with appropriate scripture
    Song of thanksgiving

Fellowship and Prayer
    Offering
    Notices
    Greeting of one another
    Prayer concerns
    Prayers for others

Preaching of the Word and the Church's Response
    Hymn
    Readings
    Prayer for illumination
    Sermon
    Prayer of response
    Hymn of commitment
    Benediction

Third Pattern

An **open service** which allows spontaneous participation may still have a definite pattern.

Praise
Songs of worship

Scripture declaring the character of God (for example, a Psalm)

Prayer of praise and confession

Songs and prayers of praise (open)

Proclamation
Readings

Sermon

Reflections and other contributions (open)

Songs of response (open)

Prayer
The congregation share concerns for others (open)

Prayer is offered (open)

Personal concerns are shared (open)

Prayer is offered (open)

Concluding songs

Prayer of dismissal

RESOURCES FOR PUBLIC WORSHIP

General

Calls to Worship and Scripture Sentences

We have come together as the family of God
in our Father's presence
to offer him praise and thanksgiving,
to hear and receive his holy word,
to bring before him the needs of the world,
to ask his forgiveness of our sins,
and to seek his grace,
that through his Son Jesus Christ
we may give ourselves to his service.

The Lord is here;
His Spirit is with us.

The Lord's love is surely not exhausted,
nor has his compassion failed;
they are new every morning,
so great is his constancy.   *Lamentations 3: 22–23*

I will celebrate your love for ever, Lord,
age after age my words shall proclaim
your faithfulness;

for I claim that love is built to last for ever
and your faithfulness founded firmly in the heavens.

Psalm 89: 1–2

Pass through the gates of God's Temple with thanks,
come into his courts with praise.
Praise him and thank him,
for the Lord is good, his devotion lasts for ever,
and his faithfulness to one generation after another.

Psalm 100: 4–5

Most Psalms offer equally suitable material.

The Word became flesh;
he made his home among us,
and we saw his glory,
such glory as befits the Father's only Son,
full of grace and truth.

John 1: 14

The nearer you go to God, the nearer he will come to
 you.
Humble yourselves before the Lord and he will lift you
 up.

James 4: 8a, 10

We proclaim Christ Jesus as Lord.
For the God who said, 'Out of darkness light shall
 shine',
has caused his light to shine in our hearts,
the light which is knowledge of the glory of God
in the face of Jesus Christ.

2 Corinthians 4: 5, 6

Invocation

May the words of my mouth and the meditation of our hearts
be pleasing in your sight, O Lord, our Rock and our Redeemer.

Psalm 19: 14

You are among us, O Lord, and we bear your name;
do not forsake us!

Jeremiah 14: 9

Lord God, we pray that as the Holy Spirit came in
wind and fire to the apostles, so he may come to us,
breathing new life into our lives, and setting our hearts
aflame with love; through Jesus Christ our Lord.

Lord Jesus Christ, you declared yourself the way, the
truth, and the life.
Reveal to us your truth, and inspire us with your life,
that now and at all times we may find in you the way
to the Father.

Living God:
in this building, used to the sound of singing;
this building which has seen baptisms and funerals;
this building where people have come to be married,
or to celebrate the birth of a child;
this building where people have wept, and been filled
with joy;
this building where people have wrestled with the deep
things of life, have prayed urgently, been stirred and
changed;

in this building where you have so often been with
your people,
be with us now.

Praise and Thanksgiving

Lord God, creator of all things,
for your love for humankind:
for your love for each person:
for the great and mysterious opportunity of life:
for the life of your Spirit within us:
for the gifts of your Spirit:
we praise and worship you; through Jesus Christ.

God, creator, we praise you
for the earth and the wonder of its life;
  for the beauty of landscape and sky;
  for the variety of seasons, animals and plants;
  for their intricate interdependence;
  and for making us to be part of it all,
  shaping landscape, affected by seasons,
  interconnected with the whole of nature.

God, inspirer, we praise you
for human history and the magnificence of our
inheritance;
  for the heights of human artistry with brush, pen,
  or chisel, fixing visions and ideas for others to share;
  for the depths of human understanding expressed
  in science, politics and daily living, enriching life
  and re-shaping society.

God, redeemer, we praise you
for Jesus Christ and the glory of your work in him;

for his life in all its fullness of doing and being;
for his following through of your way to the end;
for your raising of him and all who follow him.

For our world and all of you that it contains,
and for our life and the opportunity of living
with you that it offers,
we praise and adore you; in the name of Jesus Christ
our Lord.

God our Creator, Father and Friend, we give thanks for
the wonderful gift of life, with all its joys and
responsibilities, its experiences and opportunities.

We praise you for good health and daily food, for
the shelter and care of our homes, and the love and
loyalty of our friends.

We bless you for work honestly done, for games well
played, and for all the truth we have learned and the
good we have been able to achieve.

We thank you for the teaching and example of our
Lord Jesus Christ, for the forgiveness and salvation we
have received through him, for his presence with us
always and for the service into which he has called us.

Help us to express our thanks not only in our praises
and prayers, but also through the lives we lead;
through Jesus Christ our Lord.

Adoration

Now to him who is able to do immeasurably more
than all we ask or imagine, according to his power that
is at work among us, to him be glory in the Church
and in Christ Jesus throughout all generations, for ever
and ever! Amen.   *Ephesians 3: 20–21*

Worthy is the lamb who was slain, to receive power
and wealth and wisdom and might and honour and
glory and blessing. To him who sits on the throne and
to the lamb be blessing and honour and glory and
might for ever and ever.   *Revelation 5: 12–13*

Glory to God in the highest,
and peace to God's people on earth.

Lord God, heavenly King,
almighty God and Father,
  we worship you, we give you thanks,
  we praise you for your glory.

Lord Jesus Christ, only Son of the Father,
Lord God, Lamb of God,
you take away the sin of the world;
  have mercy on us;
you are seated at the right hand of the Father:
  receive our prayer.

For you alone are the Holy One,
you alone are the Lord,
you alone are the Most High,
  Jesus Christ,
  with the Holy Spirit,
  in the glory of God the Father. Amen.

Lord God of Hosts, who is like you?
Your strength and faithfulness, Lord, are all around
you.
You founded the world and all that is in it;
your hand is mighty, your right hand lifted high;
your throne is founded on righteousness and justice;

love and faithfulness are in attendance on you.
Happy the people who have learnt to acclaim you.
Blessed be the Lord for ever.
Amen and Amen.   *Psalms 89: 8, 11b, 13b, 14, 15a, 52*

Blessed are you, Lord God of our father Israel,
from of old and for ever.
Yours, Lord, is the greatness and the power, the glory,
the splendour, and the majesty;
for everything in heaven and on earth is yours;
yours, Lord, is the sovereignty,
and you are exalted over all as head.
Now, our God, we give you thanks
and praise your glorious name.
                              1 Chronicles 29: 10b, 11, 13

Confession

Loving God,
in the security of quiet prayer we confess to you
that we have failed to live up to the reasonable
expectations of others; we have fallen short of our own
modest standards and we are far from being all that
you would have us to be.

We have hurt our fellow men and women,
disappointed ourselves and added to your suffering.
In the name of Jesus Christ who welcomed sinners
and lifted up the downcast, we ask you to forgive us
for what we have done and what we have made of
ourselves.

Refresh our faith in your willingness to accept us,

help us enjoy our standing as your much loved
children, and enable us to live lives in which you can
take delight; through Jesus Christ our Lord.

Almighty God, our heavenly Father,
we have sinned against you and against your children,
our brothers and sisters,
in thought and word and deed,
in the evil we have done and in the good we have not
done,
through negligence, through weakness,
through our own deliberate fault.
We have wounded your love, and marred your image
in us.
We are sorry and ashamed, and repent of all our sins.
For the sake of your Son, Jesus Christ, who died for us,
forgive us all that is past;
and lead us out from darkness to walk as children of
light.

Merciful God, we confess to you now that we have
sinned.
We confess the sins that no one knows
and the sins that everyone knows:
the sins that are a burden to us
and the sins that do not bother us
because we have got used to them.
We confess our sins as a church.
We have not loved one another as Christ loved us.
We have not given ourselves in love and service for the
world
as Christ gave himself for us.
Father forgive us.
Send the Holy Spirit to us, that he may give us power

to live as, by your mercy, you have called us to live;
through Jesus Christ our Lord.

We confess that we have lived superficially.
We have pushed to the back of our minds the questions
that trouble us.
We have not found time to face the emotions that
disturb us.
We have hidden from life behind habit, activity, and
entertainments.
We have avoided you, God, even as you came after us.

In our relationships we have given less than our whole
selves
and we have not received from others what they wished
to give us of their selves.
We have countered the sharp demands of justice
with hardened hearts.
We have allowed imagination and sympathy to
wither.
Routine has been our ally and honesty our dread.

Lord God, we have shut ourselves up.
Come after us again, knock once more,
that we may open up to meet others,
rediscover ourselves, know your love, and live again.

Assurance of Forgiveness

If we claim to be sinless, we are self-deceived
and the truth is not in us. If we confess our sins,
he is just and may be trusted to forgive our sins
and cleanse us from every kind of wrongdoing.

1 John 1: 8–9

Listen—
here is good news:

'Christ Jesus came into the world to save sinners'

- to forgive you in your failure
- to accept you as you are
- to set you free from evil's power and make you
  what you were meant to be.

Listen to him,
for through him his Father says to all
who have come to him as you have come to him:

'You are accepted.
You are forgiven.
I will set you free.'

'O depth of wealth, wisdom, and knowledge in God!
How unsearchable his judgements, how untraceable his
ways! Source, Guide, and Goal of all that is—
to him be glory for ever! Amen.'   *Romans 11: 33, 36*

Prayers Before Reading or Preaching

Almighty God, in whom are hid all the treasures of
wisdom and knowledge; open our eyes that we may
behold wondrous things out of your law; and give us
grace that we may clearly understand and heartily
choose the way of your commandments; through Jesus
Christ our Lord.

O Lord and lover of humankind, cause the pure light
of your divine knowledge to shine forth in our hearts,

and open the eyes of our understanding, that we may comprehend the precepts of your gospel; through Jesus Christ our Lord.

Prayers for Ourselves

To love someone else's life more than our own;
to reach out in support of another person's weakness
when we ourselves are falling;
to give another person hope when we are close to
despair;
and to offer forgiveness when we are unforgiven;
this is what you ask of us, Lord, and it is hard:
hard to give when we are poor;
hard to help when we need help;
hard to encourage when we are discouraged.

Yet Christ loved when he was hated;
he forgave when he was crucified;
and he won eternal life for all mankind by his own
death.

We are not asked to take an untravelled way;
you have set the crucified Christ before us as risen
Lord, and promised that we can share in his life!

So, Lord, we will press on in the knowledge
that you are with us as indestructible Love,
leading us to fullness of life
which cannot be taken away from us.

Go with us, then, into the troubled and perplexed
world,
in which we too will be troubled and perplexed;
go with us and help us to calm trouble and heal
perplexity,
carrying on our shoulder the cross and in our hearts

the joy of service, until Christ's work is complete
and you are glorified for ever.

Lord, be thou within us to strengthen us,
  without us to keep us,
  above us to protect us,
  beneath us to uphold us,
  before us to direct us,
  behind us to keep us from straying,
  round about us to defend us.
Blessed be thou, O Lord our Father, for ever and ever.

Almighty God,
to whom all hearts are open,
all desires known,
and from whom no secrets are hidden:
cleanse the thoughts of our hearts
by the inspiration of your Holy Spirit,
that we may perfectly love you,
and worthily magnify your holy name;
through Christ our Lord.

Heavenly Father, we ask that we,
who have worshipped you in your Church,
may be witnesses to you in the world;
through the power of Jesus Christ our Lord.

O God of peace, sanctify us wholly;
and may we be kept in your love until the coming
of our Lord Jesus Christ.

Intercession

O God, we commend to your blessing all who suffer in mind or body according to the pattern of Christ's greater pain.

We pray for those who feel themselves forsaken or betrayed, and for people who, having worked or struggled, have nothing to show for it except the signs and penalties of failure.

We pray for the victims of injustice, for all who must endure the scorn and mockery of lesser men, and for those whose friends have all gone.

We pray for any who face a martyr's death.

We remember all who weep and thirst.

Make it true for them
that the suffering of Christ has transfigured all suffering,
that the death of Christ has transfigured all death,
and that the victory of Christ can be everyone's victory;
through his grace.

Great God, we pray for the world,
in which Jesus lived,
which he loved and taught us to love,
and for which he died.

We pray for those who are hurting—
we remember . . .
we pray for those who are fearful—
we remember . . .
we pray for those who are grieving—
we remember. . . .

Loving God, so close to these brothers and sisters for

whom we pray, may they find you in their pain, within
their fear, and sharing their sadness;
and, finding you, may they find
  healing for their hurt,
  love for their fear,
  and peace for their distress.

As Jesus, through death, came to new life for us,
so may we and those for whom we pray come to new
life:
to the glory of your name.

Loving God, we lift up in prayer the community
in which we worship, and those whose lives interweave
ours.

We pray for the other local churches: for. . . .
May their lives of worship and service be used by you,
guided by your Spirit, and may they be filled with the
joy of your risen Son; and may they, with us, be
brought into deeper partnership as we celebrate and
serve you together.

We pray for the local schools: for. . . .
May they be places where children are prized,
education valued, and the best of our society's
understanding is passed on to the future.

We pray for the places of work in this community:
for. . . .
May those who work in them find their work adds
value to their own lives and to those of others.

We pray for those whose occupation is to serve this
community: for . . .
(*e.g. health workers, police, social workers*)

May they, together with all who live here, help this to be a community where need is met and hope is given.

We pray for the town (*or district*) of——, with its own particular mix of races and ages, and its unique character and traditions.
May this be a place of compassion, justice, and vision.
May your will, Lord God, be done and your love active, in our community and in us.

Offering

To you who are our life
we give back a little of our livelihood.
To you who in Christ have given us all things
we give back this.
Together in church we share the gladness of giving.
The gifts are much or little as we have prospered much or little,
but the joy and the love and the thankfulness in which we give are one and the same.

Lord Jesus Christ, you were rich, yet for our sake you became poor, so that through your poverty we might become rich.
Accept this offering as a token of our gratitude for all you have done.

Lord God, may our offering of this portion of our money be a sign that we wish all we have and are to be used in your service.
May the use of these gifts and the living of our whole lives give you glory;
through Christ our Lord.

Creator God, maker of all things,
patient Father, awakener of our love:
accept these gifts, and our joy in offering them;
through Jesus Christ.

Lord, you judge us not by what we give,
but by what we keep.
You keep back nothing of yourself;
we offer you now all that we have and are;
through Jesus Christ our Lord.

Blessings and Benedictions

Now, Lord, you let your servant go in peace:
Your Word has been fulfilled.
My own eyes have seen the salvation
which you have prepared in the sight of every people:
a light to reveal you to the nations
and the glory of your people Israel.   *Luke 2: 29–32*

Lighten our darkness, Lord, we pray;
and in your mercy defend us
from all perils and dangers of this night;
for the love of your only Son,
our Saviour Jesus Christ.

Be the eye of God dwelling with you,
The foot of Christ in guidance with you,
The shower of the Spirit pouring on you,
Richly and generously.

The grace of the Lord Jesus Christ
and the love of God
and the partnership of the Holy Spirit
be with all of you.

The blessing of God almighty,
the Father, the Son, and the Holy Spirit,
be among you, and remain with you always.

The blessing of God, life-giver, pain-bearer,
love-maker, be with us all, now and always.

May you be strong to grasp, with all God's people,
what is the breadth and length and height and depth
of the love of Christ, and to know it, though it is
beyond knowledge. So may you attain to fullness of
being, the fullness of God himself.   *Ephesians 3: 18, 19*

The Lord's Prayer

Our Father, who art in heaven,
hallowed be thy name;
thy kingdom come;
thy will be done on earth as it is in heaven.
Give us this day our daily bread;
and forgive us our trespasses
as we forgive those who trespass against us;
and lead us not into temptation,
but deliver us from evil.
For thine is the kingdom, the power, and the
glory for ever and ever. Amen.

Our Father in heaven
hallowed be your name,
your kingdom come,
your will be done,
on earth as in heaven.
Give us today our daily bread.
Forgive us our sins
as we forgive those who sin against us.
Lead us not into temptation
but deliver us from evil.
For the kingdom, the power, and the glory are yours
now and for ever. Amen.

Worship Through The Year

A continuing ministry can provide variety of themes in worship and a comprehensive range of concerns in prayer. A sermon series or an educational syllabus will have its place, but so also will the Christian year.

Whether a lectionary of readings is followed or not, there are certain times in the year when the congregation will want to be led in worship relevant to the season. What follows attempts to show both the variety of subject matter and the way in which themes may be explored. If the cycle of the year is not followed, then themes may still be used on appropriate occasions.

The scripture references are offered as calls to worship of varying length, but they may be expanded to provide suitable readings. Further relevant passages may be found in the lectionary at the back of this book.

Each section includes brief suggestions on how the main theme might be developed through various kinds of prayers. The prayers themselves are not comprehensive but, as well as providing material for use in worship, they offer examples and starting points for exploration by those leading worship.

The sections follow the classic pattern of the Christian year, but have been given thematic titles. The three main sections focus on the trinitarian richness of God, while the themes of the subsections flow from those readings normally associated with the various seasons or special events. Thus the rhythm of our worship is determined by God and his Word.

Before Christmas

The Creator

CREATION   (Ninth Sunday before Christmas)

Genesis 1: 1–4; 2: 4b–9; Job 38: 4–7; Psalm 104: 24, 30–31; Colossians 1: 15–20; Revelation 4: 2–3, 6b–11; 21: 1–4.

Creation—the God of power—wonder—confession for misuse of the planet—prayers for farmers, foresters, environmentalists, and artists.

Praise

Creator God, we worship you. In the beginning you said, 'Let there be light' and the light shone, piercing the darkness.

You have made the vast universe and amidst its movements and glories your Spirit is at work.

Scattering the stars and moulding the hills, you have made a world full of beauty.

You have made humankind in your own image, stewards of the earth, partners in creation.

We are here because of you: that we exist is your doing. You are our God, our parent giving us life, lavishing gifts upon your children.

The distances of space praise you. The depths of our being acknowledge your creating power.

Creator God, we praise you.

FALL   (*Eighth Sunday before Christmas*)

Genesis 3: 8–10; 4: 9–10; 9: 12–17; Psalms 51: 1–4; 103: 8–13; John 3: 16–19; Romans 3: 23–24; 1 John 1: 8–10.

Confession of personal sin and communal guilt—sinfulness and injustice in human society—thanksgiving for the gospel of forgiveness—prayers for those whose lives are distorted by guilt.

Creator God, we acknowledge that we have been born into a sinful world, and confess that we have contributed to the weight of the world's sin. Forgive us, we pray.

In pride we have tried to build our own tower to heaven instead of relying on your gracious compassion.

In hatred we have divided your world into **us** and **them**, fearful for our own rights and contemptuous of the rights of others.

With indifference we have ignored the cries of the oppressed and by our own greed have added to their burdens.

In fear we have pursued our own interests while spitefully ignoring the needs of others.

All that we are and do is affected by our sinfulness; our motives are mixed and even our achievements seem flawed.

Forgive us. Remove our pride with your grace, conquer our hatred with your mercy, inspire our indifference with your suffering love, and banish our fear with the assurance of your forgiveness; through Jesus Christ our Saviour.

THE GOD WHO COMES   (*First Sunday in Advent*)

Psalms 24: 7–8; 96: 11–13; Isaiah 40: 3–5; 52: 7–10; Luke 12: 35–37a, 40; Romans 13: 11–12, 14a.

God comes to us in redemption and judgement. Prayers of greeting, confession and hope.

Praise and Greeting

Advent God, we worship you—the God who comes. You are not remote from the world you have made, but each day you come to us, blessing us with your presence.

You came in creation itself, as your Spirit moved over the waters of chaos.

You came in Jesus Christ, made flesh in our world of weakness and need.

You came in power to raise him from death, a mighty promise for all creation.

Each day you come, by your Spirit, gently and powerfully working in the lives of men and women.

At the end of time you will come, in power and righteousness, in mercy and redeeming love.

Grant us the grace to welcome your coming. Inflame our love to yearn for your presence. Enlarge our vision to recognize your coming day by day.

We greet you, Advent God.

THE GOD WHO SPEAKS *(Second Sunday in Advent)*
(Bible Sunday)

Deuteronomy 6: 4–7; 30: 11–15; Psalm 119: 97–98, 103–105; Isaiah 40: 6–8; 55: 6, 9–11; John 1: 1–5; 2 Timothy 3: 16–17; Hebrews 4: 12–13.

The Bible—praise to the God who reveals himself— confession for taking the bible for granted. Prayers for scholars, translators, preachers, and publishers.

Intercession

God of revelation,
  we thank you that you are not a silent God, isolated from humanity, leaving us to guess and speculate about the things that matter.

  We pray for those who serve you by studying manuscripts and clarifying texts;
  for scholars and preachers who wrestle with the words of life for the building up of your Church;
  for linguists, translators, and publishers who continue to serve the cause of your gospel by making the Bible available to more and more people.

  Lord, create in us a hunger for your Word,
a thankfulness for your gospel, and a faithfulness to your commands; through Jesus Christ our Lord.

THE FORERUNNER

(Third Sunday in Advent)
(Ministry)

Isaiah 6: 8–9a; 40: 3–5; 40: 9; Jeremiah 1: 4–10; Malachi
3: 1–3; Matthew 3: 1–3; 3: 11; Romans 10: 11–15;
1 Corinthians 1: 26–31.

God's preparation and call—thanksgiving for ministry and
the equipping for ministry. Prayers for those engaged in
prophetic witness and its dangers.

Intercession and Petition

God of love and truth, you call men and women to
full-time service for the building up of your Church and
the proclamation of your gospel.

We pray for local churches and associations that they
might be responsive to the leading of your Spirit, able
to recognize the gifts of ministry and the signs of your
call.

We pray for superintendents as they lead and
encourage the churches in ministry and mission, caring
for the pastors, and encouraging the people.

God of grace, you call us and you equip us for our
calling.

Open our ears to hear your call.

Open our eyes to read your Word and to see your
world as Christ sees it.

Open our hands to give what we have and what we
are back to you for your service.

Open our hearts to the wonder and the glory of your
love, that we might all minister in the way of Christ; in
his name we pray.

MARY'S FAITH   *(Fourth Sunday in Advent)*

Isaiah 7: 14; 9: 2–7; Zechariah 2: 10–11; Matthew 1: 21–23;
Luke 1: 28–33; 1: 35, 38; 1: 46–49; 1: 52–53;
1 Corinthians 1: 26–27.

Mary's faith — women — God's grace — response to God's
call — the valuing of those regarded by the world as lowly.

Thanksgiving and Dedication

Life-giving God, we thank you for calling Mary to be
the mother of Jesus.

In a world where men were in control, you chose a
young girl to nurture the Saviour of the world.

In a world where power is sought, you turned our
values upside-down by inviting Mary to share in the
great work of redemption.

We thank you that still you call women and men to
share in your saving actions.

You call us to live and serve in the way of Christ,
uncertain of the future but trusting your faithfulness.

Sometimes your choice surprises us, the way you
seem to point daunts us, your faith in our possibilities
awes us.

Help us to say 'Yes' when you call. Enlarge our
vision, strengthen our resolve and increase our sense of
your all-sufficient grace, that we might be used mightily
for your glory and for the serving of your world;
through Jesus Christ our Lord.

Christmas to Easter

The Saviour

INCARNATION (*Christmas*)

*Isaiah 9: 6–7; Luke 2: 6–7; 2: 10–11; John 1: 10–13; 1: 14;
2 Corinthians 4: 5–6; Hebrews 1: 1–2; 1 John 1: 1–2.*

*God with us—praise and thanksgiving for God alongside us
in Christ and for the opportunities for proclamation which
the season brings—prayers for peace.*

For a carol service

Loving God, we come to hear again the familiar story,
to sing the familiar songs. Break through our cosy
celebration, that we might recognize your voice and
heed your call.

Invocation

Immanuel, God with us, show us where you may be
found today: in each human birth, in family joy, in
relentless tragedy, in treasured babes, and homeless
families.

Immanuel, we rejoice that you are with us—in
everything, through everything.

Lord Christ, be born in us today.

Word of God become flesh in us that we might live
your gospel.

Light of the world shine in us and through us for the
sake of your world.

Loving God, help us to see your grace, hear your
voice, and follow in your way; through Jesus Christ
our Saviour.

NEW BEGINNINGS   (New Year)

*Deuteronomy 8: 11–14, 17–18; Joshua 1: 9; Psalm 90: 1–4;
Isaiah 55: 6–11; Luke 12: 35–37; Philippians 3: 13b–14.*

*The eternal God—prayers of praise and trust—confession for
the past and hope for the future—prayers for the leaders of
the nations.*

Thanksgiving and Trust

Lord of the ages,
you are our beginning and our end.
Everlasting God, we place our days within your care.
Eternal Father, we trust you.
For your faithfulness in the past, we thank you;
for your constant care we praise you;
for our future in your love, we place ourselves
into your keeping and offer our lives for your service;
through Jesus Christ, your eternal Son,
our Saviour.

UNITY   (The Week of Prayer for Christian Unity)
                                      (See also Pentecost)

*Matthew 5: 23–24; Mark 12: 29–31; John 13: 34–35; 17:
20–21; 1 Corinthians 10: 16–17; 12: 12–13; 2 Corinthians
5: 14–15, 17; 8: 7–9; Galatians 3: 26–28; Ephesians 2:
13–16; 2: 17–22; 4: 1–3; Colossians 1: 18–20; 1 John 4: 7–
8, 19–21.*

*The God of unity — confession for divisions in the Church —
prayers for healing, and the increasing of love and
understanding — prayers for those people and organizations
who are striving for unity — commitment to shared mission.*

Intercession

God of peace, you have shown us that your will for the
world is that all people should live in justice and peace.
You have given us a vision of hope where all humanity
lives in that wholeness of life for which we have been
created.

We pray for your world, torn apart by conflict and
fear — nations divided one from another by suspicion,
aggression, and greed, nations divided within
themselves by injustice, oppression, and powerlessness.

We pray especially for . . .

You have called your Church to be a sign of hope in a
world without hope, a healing community in a broken
world, a people of peace in a world at war with itself.

Forgive our failures of the past and create in us a
vision of unity and hope, of love and sharing, that we
might indeed be a light for the nations; through Jesus
Christ our peace.

Commitment

Lord God, we thank you
for calling us into the company
of those who trust in Christ
and seek to obey his will.

May your Spirit guide and strengthen us
in mission and service to your world;
For we are strangers no longer

but pilgrims together on the way to
your Kingdom.

DISCIPLESHIP (*Lent*)

*Deuteronomy 30: 19–20; Psalms 51: 1–4; 51: 10–11; 103: 8,
10–12; Isaiah 1: 18; 30: 15; 55: 6–7; Joel 2: 13; Micah 6:
6, 8; Matthew 16: 24–26; Romans 5: 6–8; Ephesians 6: 18;
Philippians 4: 6–7; Colossians 1: 24–27; Hebrews 10: 19–22;
1 John 1: 8–9.*

*Discipleship—identifying with Jesus through the stages of his
ministry and the journey to Jerusalem—prayers of
commitment*

Confession

Lord, remembering the depth of your love to us, we
repent of our half-hearted discipleship.
We have been called to deny ourselves:
forgive us for putting self-interest before the interests of
your kingdom;
forgive us that Christ's Lordship in our hearts has been
challenged by our ambition, our appetites, our desires,
and our needs;
forgive us for not being self-forgetful in our care for
other people.
Lord, we have been called to carry a cross:
forgive us for complaining when it has weighed heavily
upon us;
forgive us that, having received so much, we have
sacrificed so little;
forgive us for the limits we have set to Christian love;
forgive us that we have settled for mediocrity, resisting
the fire and passion of Christ's love upon the cross.

FAMILY LIFE

(*Mothering Sunday*)
(*See also fourth Sunday in Advent*)

*Genesis 17: 15–17; 1 Samuel 2: 1–3; Luke 1: 46–49; 2: 6–7;
2: 51–52; John 19: 25–27.*

*The God of love—prayers for families under stress and the
supporting services—thanksgiving for the love of God which
comes through the love of those who care for us.*

Prayer of St Anselm

And you, Jesus, sweet Lord,
are you not also a mother?
Truly, you are a mother,
the mother of all mothers,
who tasted death in your desire
to give life to your children.

For Families

God, father and mother of us all,
we pray for families in their JOY.
   Where parents are loving and children are lively;
where home is comfortable and jobs are secure,
we pray that our joy may be hallowed by thanksgiving
and our happiness increased by sharing it.
   Amid the blessings you send, keep us mindful of you,
the one who sends them.

Son of God, Saviour of all, joy and sword for Mary's
heart,
we pray for families in their SORROW.
   Where grief has come for a loved one, or where love
is no more; where jobs or home are lost or health has
failed; where neighbours or relatives make trouble and

children are wayward; where one or another is left coping with more than they bargained for, and nobody laughs, or sings.

Lord Jesus, in our desert and our Gethsemane, give us your grace of strength and peace.

Holy Spirit of unity, wisdom and love,
we pray for families in their GROWING.

Reconcile us with the fact of change in one another, and in ourselves. Teach us that love need not be unaltering in order to be constant. Show us the loveliness of the baby face grown pimply with puberty, the beauty of strong hands grown waxen-veined in age. Strengthen our relationships by contradiction and temper, as well as by acquiescence and peace.

Creator Spirit, help us grow towards mature humanity measured by nothing less than the full stature of Christ.

Father, Son and Holy Spirit, providence, grace and love:
fit our families for the life of the heavenly household, and for the service of humanity.
O Lord our God, make your way in our hearts and be glorified in the manner of our life together.

SUFFERING LOVE   (*Passion Sunday*)

Isaiah 53: 2–4; 53: 5–7; Luke 23: 33–34; Hebrews 4: 14–15;
Revelation 5: 12.

The cross and the costliness of our redemption — thanksgiving
for the gospel and God's costly love — our response in
devotion and service.

Thanksgiving and dedication

Lord Jesus,
we thank you for loving us so much that you endured
the cross for our salvation.
We thank you that amidst the pain and humiliation of
Golgotha you forgave your persecutors and prayed for
them.

Fill us with such wonder at your suffering love, that we
might long to be transformed by it.
Woo us with your costly compassion, that we might
become compassionate people, open to others in their
need.

Living Lord,
we celebrate your resurrection:
  for the way of your cross is shown to be the way of
  our salvation,
  your love and forgiveness are displayed as the keys of
  our redemption,
  and your sacrificial love is offered as the foundation of
  our hope.
Lord Jesus, help us to follow.

THE WAY OF THE CROSS   (*Palm Sunday*)

Isaiah 50: 4–9; Zechariah 9: 9; Luke 19: 37–38;
1 Corinthians 1: 20b–21; Philippians 2: 5–11.

*The servant Messiah—prayers of greeting—confession that
our hosannas turn to 'crucify'—commitment to being
pilgrims.*

Dedication

Lord Jesus, we greet your coming,
pilgrim messiah, servant king, rejected saviour.

You trod the way of a pilgrim and ascended the hill of
the Lord; you followed the path of your calling even
though Mount Zion gave way to the hill of Calvary.
Lord Jesus, help us to follow.

You rode into Jerusalem on a donkey, symbol of
humility and lowliness, mocking our dream of pomp
and glory, demonstrating the foolishness of God before
the eyes of the world.
You have shown us the way of humble service, the
way of true greatness.
Lord Jesus, help us to follow.

The cries of 'Hosanna' soon turned to 'Crucify'. The
acclamation of the crowds gave way to fear and
contempt.
You have shown us the cost of love and you have
called us to follow in your way: pilgrims of the
kingdom, living out the foolishness of God, and
trusting only in your forgiving faithfulness.
Lord Jesus, help us to follow.

THE CROSS
(Good Friday)

Psalms 22: 1–4; 40: 4–5, 10–11; 42: 8–11; 43: 5; Isaiah 42: 1–4; Romans 5: 6–8; 6: 5–11; 1 Corinthians 1: 22–25; 2 Corinthians 5: 14–17; Galatians 6: 14–16; Revelation 5: 12–13.

Confession for our sin and the sins of the world—quiet reflection and wonder at God's love and the appeal of the crucified.

Approach and Adoration

God our Father, today in remembrance and awe we tread the holy ground of Calvary:
  this place of abandonment that has become the scene of our adoration,
  this place of suffering that has become the source of our peace,
  this place of violence that has become the battlefield on which love is victorious.

Father, as we re-live the events of this day it is with awe that we count again the cost of our salvation. Words cannot be found to utter our thanksgiving. Accept our silent adoration; in Jesus' name.

RESURRECTION
(Easter Day)

1 Samuel 2: 6–8a; Psalms 16: 9–11; 30: 10–12; 73: 23–28; 118: 22–24; Hosea 6: 1–3; Matthew 12: 39–40; 28: 5–7; 28: 8–10; Mark 16: 6–7; Luke 24: 5–9; 24: 36, 45–47; John 20: 19–20; Acts 2: 22–24; 1 Corinthians 15: 3–4.

Easter day is a celebration of victory, a rejoicing at the

wonder, power, and surprise of the resurrection—prayers of
adoration and thanksgiving.

Traditional Sentences

LEADER   Christ is risen!

RESPONSE   Alleluia!

LEADER   The Lord is risen!

RESPONSE   He is risen indeed!

It is fitting that the heavens should rejoice: and that the
earth should be glad, and that the whole world, both
visible and invisible, should keep the feast.
For Christ is risen, the everlasting joy. Now all things
are filled with light, heaven, and earth, and all places
under the earth. All creation celebrates the resurrection
of Christ.

It is the day of resurrection,
Let us be glorious in splendour for the celebration, and
let us embrace one another.
Let us speak also, brothers and sisters, to those that
hate us, and in the resurrection let us forgive all things.
   So let us cry:
Christ has risen from the dead, by death trampling on
death, and has bestowed life to those who were dead.

Adoration

Living God,
we worship you today with joy in our hearts and
thanksgiving on our lips.
When the powers of evil had done their worst,
crucifying your son, and burying him in death,

you raised him to life again: an act of power giving
hope to the world.

Lord Jesus,
we rejoice that death could not keep you in its grip;
that you were raised to life, alive for evermore.
You greeted your friends and now you stand amongst
us in your risen power.

Spirit of God,
you are always giving life to the people of God,
giving birth to children of God.
Remodel us in the image of Jesus, fill us with his love
and enable us with his risen power, that we might be
faithful to his way, used by you in the redeeming of
your world.

ETERNAL LIFE   (*The season of Easter*)

*Luke 24: 29–32; John 11: 25–26; 20: 27–29; 21: 15–17;
Romans 6: 3–4; 1 Corinthians 15: 19–20; 15: 54–58;
2 Corinthians 4: 16–18; Philippians 3: 8–11; Colossians 2:
6–7, 12; Revelation 21: 3–6.*

*The weeks following Easter day provide opportunity for the
themes of life and death, hope and joy to be explored.
Prayers of praise—confidence in God's love and commitment
to life-enhancing, rather than life-denying, actions.*

Confession

God of life,
forgive our denial of life,
our destruction of its hopes,
our denial of its needs,
our distorting of its possibilities.

Fill us with your Spirit of life,
that we might be people of life,
servants of life, encouragers of life,
signs of Christ, the life of the world;
in his name we pray.

EXALTATION   (*Ascension Day and Sunday*)

*Psalms 24: 7, 10; 47: 5–7; Matthew 28: 18–20; Luke 24:
50–51; Acts 1: 11; Ephesians 1: 7–10; Philippians 2: 7b–11;
Colossians 1: 18–20; Hebrews 4: 14–16; 12: 1–2.*

*The enthronement of Christ—the uplifting of humanity
within the purposes of God—praise—prayers of dedication
to follow Christ our pioneer.*

Confession

Forgive us, Father, when we are rooted to the earth,
unable to see beyond the present, blind to the glory of
your presence. We become engrossed in what is
happening now and forget all that you yet have in store
for us.

We are so concerned with what is immediate,
temporary, and short-lived that we leave ourselves no
time for the things that are eternal and full of your
love.

Lift up our heads, Father, that we may see Christ in
all his glory and all things in their true perspective. We
ask this with the forgiveness of our sins, in your name.

Pentecost Onwards

The Spirit

THE GIFT OF THE SPIRIT (*Pentecost*)

*Genesis 1: 1–2; Isaiah 11: 1–2; 32: 15–16; 61: 1–3; Ezekiel
37: 9–10; Joel 2: 28; Mark 1: 9–13; John 4: 23–24;
14: 15–17; 16: 13–14; Acts 2: 1–4; 1 Corinthians 12: 4–7;
14: 12; Ephesians 6: 18; 1 Peter 2: 9.*

*The gift of the Holy Spirit—the Pentecost story—empowering
for mission—unifying all people—gifts of prophecy—praise
and thanksgiving—confession of our lack of expectancy—
prayers for the Church—its fellowship and its mission.*

Confession

Spirit of God,
you are the breath of creation,
the wind of change that blows through our lives,
opening us up to new dreams, and new hopes,
new life in Jesus Christ.

Forgive us our closed minds
which barricade themselves against new ideas,
preferring the past to what you might want to do
through us tomorrow.

Forgive us our closed eyes
which fail to see the needs of your world,
blind to opportunities of service and love.

Forgive us our closed hands
which clutch our gifts and our wealth for our own use
alone.

Forgive us our closed hearts
which limit our affections to ourselves and our own.

Spirit of new life,
forgive us and break down the prison walls of our
selfishness,
that we might be open to your love
and open for the service of your world;
through Jesus Christ our Lord.

Intercession

Lord God,
today we celebrate the birthday of the Church.
The followers of Jesus waited behind locked doors, yet
your Spirit came to them in power, changing them
from a bewildered band into a proclaiming people.

We pray for ourselves and for your whole Church,
that we might be open to the empowering presence of
your Spirit, open to the gracious gifting of your Spirit,
and open to the adventurous leading of your Spirit.

Holy Spirit, as you filled those first Christians with
an enthusiasm for the gospel of Christ, so enthuse us,
that we go out into the streets and market places of our
world, preaching the good news of Jesus Christ.

Holy Spirit, all who heard the apostles' preaching
understood in their own language. Fill us with a vision
of the whole earth filled with your glory. Send us out
to all people, of every race and colour, rich and poor,
powerful and oppressed, that we might be messengers
of the gospel and servants of your kingdom.

Holy Spirit, that first Christian community began
a life of sharing in worship and in living. Fill us with
a generous spirit, ready to share what we are and what
we have with others. Break down our pride that we

might have the grace to receive from the riches of others.

Holy Spirit, God with us, fill your people with power and love, vision and purpose that we might be agents of your gospel for the whole world; through Jesus Christ our Lord.

THE RICHES OF GOD   (*Trinity Sunday*)

Matthew 28: 19; John 14: 7–11; 14: 26–27; 16: 12–15; 17: 1–5; Romans 1: 2–4; 2 Corinthians 13: 14; Ephesians 4: 4–6; 1 Peter 1: 1a, 2; Jude 20b–21.

The wonder and mystery of God—fellowship in God— prayers of praise, wonder, offering—prayers for unity and the healing of divisions.

Intercession

Lord Jesus Christ, you said that you were one with the Father and you gave your Spirit to the disciples, offering them your peace; we pray for the unity of your Church and the peace of your world.

Lord God, forgive us the fears and suspicions, the half truths and ignorance which reinforce our divisions.

We pray that your Spirit of truth will open our minds so that we might learn from one another.

We pray that your Spirit of love will fill our hearts so that we might forgive and encourage one another.

We pray that your Spirit of unity will work in our lives, binding us together in you, our only God, Father, Son, and Holy Spirit.

We pray for your world, broken into hostile camps by fear, hatred, suspicion, greed, and the pursuit of power.

We pray for all those who are working for peace and

understanding, the reconciling of conflicts, and the healing of divisions.

We pray for those who are caring for the casualties of conflict, used by your love in caring for the downtrodden and oppressed.

We pray for those who are leaders in communities, that they might lead with wisdom and in a spirit of service.

We pray that the search for unity in your Church might serve the search for unity in our divided world, for there is one God and Father of all, who is over all, and through all, and in all.

CHURCH ANNIVERSARY

Genesis 12: 1; Deuteronomy 6: 4–9; 30: 11–15; Psalm 90: 1–2; Isaiah 49: 5–6; 51: 1–3; Acts 2: 42–47; 1 Corinthians 1: 26–31; 10: 16–17; 12: 4–7; 14: 26; 15: 1–2, 2 Corinthians 4: 5–9; 5: 16–18; Ephesians 3: 14–19; 4: 1–6; Philippians 2: 1–5; Hebrews 11: 1–2, 8–10; 12: 1–2; 12: 18a, 22–24a; 1 Peter 2: 9–10; 1 John 1: 5–7; Revelation 7: 9–10.

Thanksgiving for the past and the hope of faithfulness in the future — thankfulness for those who have passed on the faith to us — prayers for the fellowship of the church and its responsiveness to God's will in its life and mission — dedication and trust.

Dedication

Lord, how strange it is that you should call us to be your Church, yet you have always worked through women and men in the working out of your purpose. Through prophets and disciples, leaders and followers,

preachers and listeners, you have called people, that
your redeeming love would work through them.

Above all, in Jesus your Word has become flesh and
a human being has lived your will. He has died for us
and you have raised him for us, that he might be our
foundation and our head. Fill us with his love that we
might truly be his disciples.

We dedicate ourselves now to being your people.
Accept our worship and our prayers, our intentions and
our gifts. All has come from you and now, as we pray,
your Spirit prompts us and empowers us. Grant us
your grace that we might be faithful to our calling as
your Church. Deepen our faith, strengthen our love,
and increase our hope that we might be an offering
acceptable to you and available for your will; through
Jesus Christ our Lord.

HARVEST

*Genesis 1: 11–12; 1: 26–31; 8: 22; Deuteronomy 8: 11–14,
16–18; 16: 16b–17; Psalm 24: 1; 65: 9–13; 104: 24, 27–28;
107: 8–9; 145: 14–16; Hosea 6: 1–3; Joel 2: 23–24; Amos 5:
10–15; Micah 6: 8; 6: 9–12; Mark 4: 26–29; Luke 12: 15;
2 Corinthians 8: 1–2, 8–9; 9: 6–9.*

*Celebration of creation — confession for the misuse of the
planet and the unjust distribution of wealth — prayers for
those who grow food and produce wealth — thanksgiving and
commitment to good stewardship.*

Thanksgiving and dedication

God our Father,
    We thank you today
for the splendour and beauty of creation;

for the ordered succession of seasons;
for your love which made the world.
    We thank you for the good and fertile earth;
for the fruits of the earth in their seasons;
for the life that sustains our life;
for the food that we daily enjoy.
    We thank you for those whose labour supplies our
physical needs; for those who harvest crops, those who
transport them, those who process them, those who sell
them.

Our God, we thank you for the gift of yourself
in Jesus, our Saviour and Lord;
for his living, dying, and rising again
in your loving redemption of the world.

We thank you, our God,
for your Holy Spirit, the giver of life;
for the Church, a foretaste of your new creation,
and for our privilege in being part of it.

Loving God, we thank you for your mighty acts in the
creation and redemption of the world; and we offer
ourselves to you in gratitude, that we may serve you
and our fellow men and women joyfully and faithfully
throughout our lives; in the name of Jesus Christ our
Lord.

Intercession

Loving Lord, we pray for those who have no harvest to
celebrate, no crops to gather, or labour to pursue.
    We pray for those who live on land that is hard to
farm, scratching out a living in a hostile soil, amidst
rocky ground and scorching earth.
    We pray for those who scratch no living from the

earth, where the whole world seems to squeeze the life from their bodies.

We pray for those who have left their homes, driven by war or want to become refugees, aliens dependent on others.

We pray for those without work: women and men made redundant by changing needs, children living off their wits in the streets of sprawling cities.

We pray for those with no energy for praise, whose bread is bitterness and whose water is tears.

We confess our part in the sin of the world and pray that you might grant us a vision of justice as well as charity and strengthen our readiness to change as well as to help; through Jesus Christ our Lord.

ONE WORLD WEEK

Genesis 1: 26–28; 2: 7–8; 9: 12–16; Exodus 3: 7–8a, 10; Psalms 24: 1–2; 100; Isaiah 60: 1–3; Micah 4: 1–4; Matthew 25: 37–40; Luke 4: 18–19; John 12: 31–32; Acts 10: 34–36; Galatians 3: 14; Ephesians 3: 14–19; 1 John 4: 19–21.

All the earth is the Lord's—all people are his children—the unity of humanity within the purposes of God—thanksgiving for the variety of cultures and traditions—prayers for the World Council of Churches, for peace, for reconciliation, and the healing of the nations.

Intercession

God of hope, you have given the rainbow as a symbol of your faithfulness:
　in its colours, you have shown us the variety of human life and your call to unity;

its span between heaven and earth remind us that our hopes for the future are founded on your grace;
   you have turned your face from judgement to redemption and have called us to be peacemakers;

We pray for people whose humanity is denied by others;
   for those persecuted or imprisoned because of their religion or their politics;
   for those who try to oppress and manipulate others and in so doing lose sight of their own humanity;
   for those who work for peace and justice, whatever the cost.

Lord God, make us your rainbow people, glorying in our God-given variety, passionate for peace, trusting in your grace; in the name of Jesus Christ, the hope of the world.

WORLD MISSION

Psalms 67: 1–3; 96: 7–10a; Isaiah 6: 8; Jeremiah 1: 4–8; Matthew 9: 35–38; 28: 18–20; Mark 16: 15–16a; Luke 10: 8–9; John 8: 12; 10: 16; 20: 21; Acts 13: 2–3; 17: 24–27a; Romans 10: 13–15; 1 Corinthians 9: 19–23.

The world-wide mission of the church—partnership between Christians of different countries—prayers for those who leave their own land to serve the gospel elsewhere—prayers for the world church, the Baptist Missionary Society, and its partners.

Thanksgiving

Eternal God,
Creator of all, Saviour of all, Lord of all,
we thank you that your love and power encompass all things and all people.

As the universal creator, the whole universe is in
your hands: there is no part of this earth that does not
belong to you.

As our Saviour and Lord, there are no people beyond
your redeeming love.

We thank you that in all countries there are witnesses
to your gospel, bearing testimony through their words
and actions to the good news of Jesus Christ.

We thank you for your Church in each place, for
your Spirit equipping it with gifts and empowering
your people to proclaim the good news of Jesus Christ.

We thank you for Christian partnership across
continents and national boundaries, for those who have
responded to your call to serve the Church in a land
that is not their own.

Grant that we may be worthy of this great company
of saints, ready to witness and serve in the name of our
Lord Christ.

REMEMBRANCE SUNDAY

*Deuteronomy 7: 9; 2 Samuel 1: 21, 27; Psalms 46: 1–3; 46:
10–11; 67: 1–2; 90: 1–4, 12–14; Isaiah 25: 4–5; 25: 6–8;
John 12: 24; 12: 31–32; Romans 8: 38–39; Hebrews 12:
1–2; Revelation 7: 9–12.*

*Remembrance of those who have served and died in war—
prayers for peace and for those who work for peace—for the
victims of war—civilians, refugees, and all brutalized by
violence.*

Appropriate Sentences

The righteous man, though he die early, will be at rest.
For old age is not honoured for length of time, not

measured by number of years; but understanding is grey hair for men, and a blameless life is ripe old age.

The righteous live for ever and their reward is with the Lord; the Most High takes care of them. Therefore they will receive a glorious crown and a beautiful diadem from the hand of the Lord, because with his right hand he will cover them and with his arm he will shield them.

Commemoration

Friends, let us remember in silence before God, all those who have died in war.

THE TWO MINUTES SILENCE

They shall grow not old, as we that are left grow old.
Age shall not weary them, nor the years condemn.
At the going down of the sun and in the morning
we will remember them.

Almighty Father, you call your children to live as brothers and sisters in love and harmony, and have given your Son to be our Saviour, the Prince of Peace; grant that we, who are called by his name, may yield our lives to your service, and strive for reconciliation, understanding, and peace in all our relationships; for the sake of Jesus Christ our Lord.

Intercession

Father of mercies and God of all comfort, we pray this day for all those who continue to suffer because of war:

the widows, orphans, and all who are bereaved;
the wounded, crippled, deaf, dumb, and blinded;
the shell-shocked and mentally deranged;
the refugees without home, work, or country.
Grant to them all your healing and strength, your help
and consolation, and let it be mediated wherever
possible through us; for Jesus Christ's sake.

THE LORD'S SUPPER

Three patterns of the Lord's Supper are offered, supported by notes and suggestions. Each contains material which may be used as set out here, interchanged, or incorporated into other patterns of worship.

Each pattern expresses a Baptist understanding of the Lord's Supper, emphasizing the gathered congregation seated around the Lord's Table, the participation of lay people, and the sharing of pastoral concerns with prayers for the fellowship.

The Supper is inseparable from the Word, and should always be preceded by the declaration of the Gospel. If the service begins with the Invitation, as is sometimes the case at occasional communion services, then the reading of scripture and an exposition, however brief, should be included. The Word needs to be broken as well as the bread.

There is a need for clear words of invitation. This is important as a reminder that the Table is the Lord's and the invitation is his. Our sharing in this meal is sheer grace and does not rest on our goodness or attainments.

Former practice marked a separation of the Lord's Supper from the Service of the Word with a definite break, out of a desire that only believers took part in the Supper. More recent practice has emphasized the unity of Word and Sacrament, but may have led to a situation where some people remain at the service without being able to enter into its meaning wholeheartedly. It is pastorally wise, therefore, to precede the Supper with some statement as to its meaning and how to respond.

'The Breaking of Bread' was an early title for the Lord's Supper (see Luke 24: 35) and as an action will have different significance for different people. It may be seen as the necessary preparation for sharing, a sign of the violent cost of our salvation, or the completeness of Christ's self-offering and the complete self-offering to which we are called. The symbolism of the action is heightened if one loaf is used (see 1 Corinthians 10: 17). However, should local custom insist on fragments of bread being prepared previously, there should still be a large piece of bread for this moment in the service.

The lifting of the cup in full view of the congregation corresponds to the breaking of the bread. It is of particular importance in those fellowships where there has been a return to the use of a common cup, but it is also appropriate when individual glasses are to be used for the distribution to the congregation, as it links what is happening to the account of the Last Supper which, through the Words of Institution, provides the narrative framework for what is said and done.

There is some variety amongst Baptists over who will preside at the Lord's Supper. Usually it will be the person invited by the local Church Meeting to do so. When there is a minister, he or she will usually be that person, but it may be a lay pastor, lay preacher or deacon. It is a great privilege and honour to preside at the table, and we are able to do so only because of the calling of Christ through his Church—whether that calling be a life-time one of ordained ministry or the calling of a local church with a temporary need. The word 'minister' has been used throughout this order, but is used for the sake of simplicity, not in an attempt to restrict the leading of 'The Lord's Supper'.

First Pattern

This approach to the Lord's Supper gives as much time to silence as possible, focusing on the words of Jesus, 'Do this in remembrance of me'. The word 'remembrance' means more than a personal recalling of past events. It is a making present to the gathered congregation the events of the cross and resurrection. The Supper is the church setting itself once again under the cross. Furthermore, in the breaking of bread and the sharing of the cup, the disciples' eyes are opened to the presence of the risen Christ, who gives to each believer the fruits of his sacrifice upon the cross. Too much elaboration or wordiness must not be allowed to obscure this central emphasis.

> Call to worship
> Hymn of praise
> Prayer
> Bible reading(s)
> Sermon
> Hymn
> Prayers for the world,
>   the Church, and ourselves
> The offering of gifts
> Prayer of dedication
> Invitation to the Table
> Prayer of preparation *and/or* confession
> Hymn
> Reception of new members
> News of the fellowship

Prayers for the fellowship
  (*or later, as desired*)

Gospel words

Institution

Thanksgiving for the bread and wine[1]

Breaking of bread and distribution

Sharing the cup

Prayer of thanksgiving and prayers for the
  fellowship, missionaries, and the world church

Hymn

Benediction

---

[1] The Prayer of Thanksgiving centres on those mighty acts of God whereby our redemption was accomplished. It is a recalling of the Passion story when our Lord was lifted up in suffering and glory, and a looking forward in hope to the final victory of love. It is a thanksgiving for the bread and wine which are symbols of the grace of our Lord Jesus Christ. This prayer calls upon the Holy Spirit, that by his presence in their hearts the people may enter into the meaning of the bread and the wine, draw near to the risen Christ, and receive him afresh. It concludes with a fitting response of love, gratitude, and re-consecration.

Second Pattern

This pattern is a Baptist response to liturgical concerns which are wider than one section of the Church. For example, the treatment of The Peace is an attempt to allow this relatively recent emphasis to interact with a Baptist view of fellowship and its place in the Lord's Supper.

Our Praise

> Call to worship
> Hymn
> Prayers of praise and confession
> Assurance of forgiveness
> Family time
> (*Sharing the theme with all ages*)

God's Word

> Old Testament reading
> New Testament reading
> Hymn
> Sermon

Our Response

> Hymn
> Prayers of intercession and thanksgiving
> Offering of gifts

Prayer of dedication[1]

The Lord's Supper

Invitation to the table

Communion hymn

Gospel words

Prayer of preparation or confession[2]

The Peace[3]

Institution

Thanksgiving

The breaking of bread

Sharing the bread

The lifting of the cup

Sharing of wine

[1] This prayer will dedicate the gifts of money and lives which are the congregation's response to God. It may also look forward by offering the bread and wine in a prayer which presents all these things to God for him to bless and use. If desired, the bread and wine may be brought to the table when the offering of money is brought forward.

[2] Before we share the bread and wine, there should be opportunity for the confession of our sins. If this has not happened earlier in the service, then it could do so here.

[3] 'The Peace' reminds us that the theme of reconciliation runs through the Lord's Supper. Bread and wine point to the cost of our reconciliation to God and we are called to be at peace with one another (see Matthew 5: 23–25). Informal greetings, or formal words of response between members of the congregation, or simply an acclamation of peace announced by the minister, focus on the healing of the people of God and the ministry of reconciliation to which we are called.

Because of this emphasis on fellowship, some may wish to welcome new members or share news and prayer at this point.

Prayer or words of acclamation

Hymn

Words of commissioning,
dismissal and blessing[4]

[4] Just as the Supper looks forward to the final consummation of
the purposes of God, so the meal ends with an 'outward' emphasis.
Empowered by the Spirit, the people of God are sent back into the
world to live and speak the mission of God.

Third Pattern

This pattern is offered for those who set the Lord's Supper within a more informal and participatory approach to worship.

Call to worship

Hymn of praise

Prayers of adoration and confession

Some members of the congregation may be invited to read from a psalm appropriate verses which exalt and praise God.

Songs may be sung which concentrate on the birth, life, death, and resurrection of Jesus

Readings from the Old and New Testaments

Prayer for illumination

Sermon

Prayer of response

Song of commitment

Words of invitation, such as:

> **Brothers and sisters in Christ, it is right that we call to mind the meaning of the Lord's Supper. It is a remembrance of the cross, an encounter with the risen Lord, a communion with one another in his body, and an anticipation of his coming.**

Read 1 Corinthians 11: 23–26

Members of the congregation may be invited to offer

one-sentence prayers of thanksgiving for God's mighty acts in Jesus.

The leader gives the bread to the servers and the congregation serve one another with the words,

> **'This is the body of Christ, broken for you'.**

A modern version of the Lord's Prayer may be said to emphasize unity in the body of Christ.

The wine is then served in a similar way with the words,

> **'This is Christ's blood shed for you'.**

The congregation may be invited to offer brief prayers of praise or to choose a chorus to be sung which concentrates on the risen or exalted Lord.

The emphasis now focuses on the fellowship of believers:

the Peace may be given;
new members may be received;
news of the fellowship may be shared;
prayers for healing may be sought;
words of testimony and encouragement may be invited;
prayers may be offered for absent members,
  the wider Church, and the world.

Final hymn of triumph

The Grace said together

The Lord's Supper

First Pattern

Invitation to the Table

The Table of the Lord is spread. It is for those who will come and see in broken bread and poured out wine symbols of his life shed for us on the cross and raised again on the third day. The Risen Christ is present among his people and it is here that we meet him. It is for those who know him a little and long to know him more. We invite all who are seeking him and all who are weary of their sin and doubt to come and share in the feast. If you do not feel able to take a full part, you are welcome to remain among us without receiving the bread and wine.

> *Or:*

Brothers and sisters in Christ, it is right that we call to mind the meaning of this Supper. It is a remembrance of the sacrifice of Christ for the sin of the world; an encounter with the risen Lord; a feeding on him in faith; a communion with one another in his body, the Church; and a looking forward to the day when he will come again. Therefore, we need to come in faith, conscious of our weakness, renouncing our sin, humbly putting our trust in Christ, and seeking his grace.

Prayer of Preparation

> *(and a prayer of confession if not already included earlier in the service)*

Hymn

(Those who are to assist the minister take their place at the Table and any who wish to leave may do so at this point)

Reception of New Members

News of the Fellowship

Prayers for the Fellowship *(or later as desired)*

Gospel Words

A selection of the following, or other suitable scriptures, is read:

How shall I repay the Lord for all his benefits to me? I will take up the cup of salvation and call upon the name of the Lord. I will pay my vows to the Lord in the presence of all his people.   *Psalm 116: 12*

We had all strayed like sheep, each of us had gone his own way; but the Lord laid upon him the guilt of us all. He was pierced for our transgressions, tortured for our iniquities; the chastisement he bore is health for us, and by his scourging we are healed.   *Isaiah 53: 6, 5*

God loved the world so much that he gave his only Son, that everyone who has faith in him may not die but have eternal life.   *John 3: 16*

Christ died for us while we were yet sinners, and that is God's own proof of his love towards us.   *Romans 5: 8*

I am that living bread which has come down from heaven; if anyone eats this bread he shall live for ever. Moreover, the bread which I will give is my own flesh; I give it for the life of the world. *John 6: 51*

Come to me, all you who are weary and burdened, and I will give you rest. Take my yoke upon you and learn from me, for I am gentle and humble in heart, and you will find rest for your souls. *Matthew 11: 28–29*

Here I stand knocking at the door; if anyone hears my voice and opens the door, I will come in and sit down to supper with him and he with me. *Revelation 3: 20*

For you did not receive a spirit that makes you a slave again to fear, but you received the Spirit of sonship. And by him we cry, 'Abba, Father'. The Spirit himself testifies with our spirit that we are God's children.

Romans 8: 15–16

Institution

For I received from the Lord what I also passed on to you: The Lord Jesus, on the night he was betrayed, took bread, and when he had given thanks, he broke it and said, 'This is my body, which is for you; do this in remembrance of me.' In the same way, after supper he took the cup, saying, 'This cup is the new covenant in my blood; do this, whenever you drink it, in remembrance of me.' For whenever you eat this bread and drink this cup, you proclaim the Lord's death until he comes. *1 Corinthians 11: 23–26*

Or:

The disciples did as Jesus had directed them and
prepared the Passover. When evening came, Jesus was
reclining at the table with the Twelve. And while they
were eating, he said, 'I tell you the truth, one of you
will betray me.' They were very sad and began to say
to him one after the other, 'Surely not I, Lord?' While
they were eating, Jesus took bread, gave thanks and
broke it, and gave it to his disciples, saying, 'Take and
eat; this is my body.' Then he took the cup, gave
thanks and offered it to them, saying, 'Drink from it,
all of you. This is my blood of the covenant, which is
poured out for many for the forgiveness of sins. I tell
you, I will not drink of this fruit of the vine from now
on until that day when I drink it anew with you in my
Father's kingdom.'   *Matthew 26: 19–22, 26–29*

Thanksgiving

Breaking of Bread and Distribution

> (*A loaf is broken and shared among the
> plates, which are given to the deacons who
> serve the people. The minister then serves
> the deacons.*)

Jesus said, 'This is my body, which is for you; do this
in remembrance of me.'

> *Silence*

Sharing the Cup

> *The minister says:*

In the same way, after supper he took the cup.

*After the distribution of the wine, the
minister says:*

Jesus said, 'This cup is the new covenant in my blood;
do this, whenever you drink it, in remembrance of me.'

Silence

Some, or all, of the following:

The Lord's Prayer

Prayer of Thanksgiving *for the blessings received at the
Table.*

Prayer for the Fellowship (*recalling those mentioned earlier,
any missionaries, and the world-wide
Church*)

Hymn

Benediction

The Lord's Supper

Second Pattern

Invitation to the Table

*The minister may now be joined at the Table by
the deacons or whoever is going to share in the
distribution of the bread and the wine.*

*If newly baptized members or those called to
exercise a ministry in the church are to receive the*

laying on of hands, it may be administered with
prayer at this point.

Here also, or before the sharing of the peace,
new members may be welcomed and received
with the right hand of fellowship and with prayer
offered.

If you truly and earnestly repent of your sins, and are
in love and charity with your neighbours, and are
resolved to lead a new life, following the
commandments of God, and walking henceforth in his
holy ways: draw near with faith, and take this
sacrament to your comfort and growth in grace.

Come to this sacred table, not because you must but
because you may; come not to testify that you are
righteous, but that you sincerely love our Lord Jesus
Christ, and desire to be his true disciples; come, not
because you are strong, but because you are weak; not
because you have any claim on heaven's rewards, but
because in your frailty and sin you stand in constant
need of heaven's mercy and help.

   Or:

Come to this table, not because you must but because
you may, not because you are strong, but because you
are weak.
Come, not because any goodness of your own gives
you a right to come, but because you need mercy and
help.
Come, because you love the Lord a little and would
like to love him more.
Come, because he loved you and gave himself for you.
Come and meet the risen Christ, for we are his Body.

Or:

Behold: the gifts of God for the people of God!

Now that the Supper of the Lord is spread before you, lift up your minds and hearts above all faithless fears and cares; let this bread and wine be to you the witnesses and signs of the grace of our Lord Jesus Christ, the love of God and the fellowship of the Holy Spirit. Consecrate your lives afresh to God and pray for strength and grace to do and bear his holy will.

Communion Hymn

Gospel Words

> *A passage of scripture may now be read, or one or more of the following:*

'I am the bread of life,' Jesus told them. 'Whoever comes to me will never be hungry; whoever believes in me will never be thirsty.'   *John 6: 35*

I am the living bread that has come down from heaven; if anyone eats this bread, he will live for ever. The bread which I shall give is my own flesh, given for the life of the world.   *John 6: 51*

Jesus said, 'Listen! I stand at the door and knock; if any hear my voice and open the door, I will come into the house and eat with them, and they with me.'
> *Revelation 3: 20*

When we bless 'the cup of blessing', is it not a means of sharing in the blood of Christ? When we break the

bread, is it not a means of sharing in the body of
Christ? Because there is one loaf, we, many as we are,
are one body; for we all share one loaf.

1 Corinthians 10: 16–17

Prayer of Preparation or Confession

*There may follow a prayer of confession, if one
has not been offered earlier, or a prayer of
preparation, such as:*

Almighty God,
to whom all hearts are open,
all desires known,
and from whom no secrets are hidden:
cleanse the thoughts of our hearts
by the inspiration of your Holy Spirit,
that we may perfectly love you,
and worthily magnify your holy name;
through Christ our Lord.

Or:

Lord, we come to your table trusting in your mercy
and not in any goodness of our own.
We are not worthy even to gather up the crumbs under
your table, but it is your nature always to have mercy,
and on that we depend.
So feed us with the body and blood of Jesus Christ,
your Son, that we may for ever live in him and he
in us.

The Peace

*If not received earlier, new members may now be
welcomed and received with the right hand of
fellowship and prayer. Some of the following*

sentences may be said responsively or read by the minister as an acclamation.

As this bread, once scattered over the hills, was brought together and became one loaf, so, Lord, may your Church be united and brought together from the ends of the earth into your Kingdom.

LEADER   Christ is our peace.
          He has reconciled us to God in one body
          by the cross.

RESPONSE We meet in his name and share his peace.

    Or:

LEADER   We are the Body of Christ.
          In the one Spirit we were baptized into
          one body.

RESPONSE Let us then pursue all that makes for
          peace and builds up our common life.

This may be followed by the greeting:

LEADER   The peace of the Lord be always with you

RESPONSE and also with you.

The minister may then invite the members of the congregation to greet one another with a sign of peace and with words such as those above or:

GREETING Christ is our peace:

RESPONSE Let us live in his love.

If desired, prayers for the church family may be offered here.

Institution

The minister may wish to lift, or point to, the bread and the wine when they are mentioned in the words of institution.

The apostle Paul tells us of the institution of the Lord's Supper:

For the tradition which I handed on to you came to me from the Lord himself: that on the night of his arrest the Lord Jesus took bread, and after giving thanks to God broke it and said: 'This is my body, which is *(broken)* for you; do this in memory of me.' In the same way, he took the cup after supper, and said: 'This cup is the new covenant sealed by my blood. Whenever you drink it, do this in memory of me.' For every time you eat this bread and drink the cup, you proclaim the death of the Lord, until he comes.

1 Corinthians 11: 23–26

Thanksgiving

One of the following prayers may be offered or extempore prayer, which should include THANKSGIVING for all God has done in creation and redemption and for bread and wine which focus this redemption in the death and resurrection of Jesus Christ 'until he comes'. The prayer should end with an INVOCATION, calling on the Spirit to transform and empower his people, as they gather and receive bread and wine, equipping them for service.

Eternal God and Father, we offer you our praise and thanksgiving:

for the creation of your world in all its richness and
glory;
for your gracious work of redemption in liberating
the oppressed, renewing the weary and forgiving the
sinful;
for your calling of men and women to share in the
work of salvation in the story of Israel and our
story;
for Jesus Christ our Lord, the eternal Word made
flesh, sharing our humanity and revealing your love
and compassion;
for his life and ministry in word and action, his
lifting up of the lowly and his healing of the broken;
for his redeeming death on the cross for all
humanity, of which this bread and this cup are the
symbol and sign.

We thank you for raising him to life again and exalting
him so that we might call him 'Lord', as we offer him
our allegiance and seek to share his way.

We thank you for the gift of your Holy Spirit,
powerfully present in your people and your world, for
the fellowship of your church, for all the means of
grace and the hope of glory.

Living God, fill us with your Spirit, that as we share
this bread and this wine we may feed on the body and
blood of Christ, and be empowered for service in your
world.

Accept our prayers and thanksgiving in the name of
Jesus Christ, the light of the world and the life of your
people.

Or:

LEADER	Lift up your hearts.
RESPONSE	We lift them to the Lord.
LEADER	Let us give thanks to the Lord our God.
RESPONSE	It is right to give him thanks and praise.
LEADER	It is not only right, it is our duty and our joy, at all times and in all places, to give you thanks and praise, holy Father, heavenly king, almighty and eternal God, through Jesus Christ, your only Son, our Lord.

Here may follow extempore or open prayer . . .

LEADER	Therefore with angels and archangels, and with all the company of heaven, we proclaim your great and glorious Name, for ever praising you and saying:
RESPONSE	Holy, Holy, Holy, God of power and might, Heaven and earth are full of your glory. Hosanna in the highest! Blessed is he who comes in the name of the Lord! Hosanna in the highest!

The Breaking of Bread

The bread may now be lifted and broken with the words:

Jesus said, 'This is my body which is broken for you; do this in memory of me.'

Sharing the Bread

> *When the minister has broken the bread and*
> *placed a portion on each plate, the bread shall be*
> *distributed with words such as:*

When we break the bread, is it not a means of sharing
in the body of Christ? Because there is one loaf, we,
though many, are one body; for it is one loaf of which
we all partake.   *1 Corinthians 10: 16–17*

> *Or:*

Take this in remembrance that Christ died for you and
feed on him in your heart by faith with thanksgiving.

The Lifting of the Cup

> *The cup may now be raised in full view of the*
> *congregation with such words as:*

How can I repay the Lord for all his benefits to me?
I shall lift up the cup of salvation and call on the Lord
by name.
I shall pay my vows to the Lord in the presence of all
his people.   *Psalm 116: 12–14*

> *Or:*

In the same way he took the cup after supper, and said:
'This cup is the new covenant sealed by my blood.
Whenever you drink it, do this in memory of me.'
                                          1 Corinthians 11: 25

> *Or:*

Drink this and remember that Christ's blood was shed
for you and be thankful.

Sharing the Wine

If individual glasses are used and the wine is retained to be drunk together, then the minister, when all are ready to drink, may use one of the sentences above or other appropriate words.

Prayer or Words of Acclamation

After all have received the wine and after a period of silence, sentences and prayers may be used, such as:

LEADER   Your death, O Lord, we commemorate.
Your resurrection we confess.
Your final coming we await.
Glory be to you, O Christ.

RESPONSE   Christ has died.
Christ is risen.
Christ will come again.

Or:

Almighty God,
we thank you for feeding us
with the body and blood of your Son Jesus Christ.
Through him we offer you our souls and bodies
to be a living sacrifice.
Send us out
in the power of your Spirit
to live and work
to your praise and glory.

Or:

Father of all, we give you thanks and praise, that when
we were still far off you met us in your Son and

brought us home. Dying and living, he declared your love, gave us grace, and opened the gate of glory.
May we who share Christ's body live his risen life;
   we who drink his cup bring life to others;
   we whom the Spirit lights give light to the world.
Keep us firm in the hope you have set before us, so we and all your children shall be free, and the whole earth live to praise your name; through Christ our Lord.

> *Or:*

Most gracious God, we praise you for what you have given and for what you have promised us here. You have made us one with all your people in heaven and on earth. You have fed us with the bread of life and renewed us for your service.
Now we give ourselves to you and we ask that our daily living may be part of the life of your kingdom, and that our love may be your love reaching out into the life of the world;
through Jesus Christ our Lord.

Hymn

Words of Commissioning, Dismissal and Blessing

Go into God's world with joy, and peace, and love, and hope in your hearts;
and the blessing of almighty God, creator, redeemer, and sustainer, be with you all.

> *Or:*

Love with all sincerity;
hate what is evil;
cling to what is good;

be joyful in hope,
patient in affliction,
faithful in prayer.
Bless those who persecute you;
bless and do not curse.
Rejoice with those who rejoice
and mourn with those who mourn.
Live in harmony with one another.
Do not repay anyone evil for evil.

And the blessing of God,
Father, Son, and Holy Spirit,
be with you all.   *From Romans 12: 9–17*

THE BAPTISM OF BELIEVERS AND RECEPTION INTO MEMBERSHIP

Believers' baptism, reception into membership at the Lord's Supper, and the laying on of hands, all relate to our one initiation into the Body of Christ. These elements may take place within a single act of worship, or they may be divided between morning and evening services, or two Sundays. There is further variety in that those churches which practise the laying on of hands place it differently within the sequence: it may happen in the baptistry, or before or after reception into membership. Reception into membership is not, of course, always linked directly with baptism, but may follow professions of faith and transfer from another church.

To accommodate these variations, this section includes two patterns for the whole process of Christian initiation, followed by material for each of the elements in that process.

First Pattern

Baptism and the Lord's Supper

Call to worship

Hymn

Prayer of praise and confession

Reading

Sermon

Hymn

Baptism   Introduction

                Questions to the candidate(s)

                Prayer

                Baptism

leader and newly baptized leave to change

Hymn

Prayers of response and intercession

Offering

leader and newly baptized re-enter
newly baptized may bring bread and wine to the
Table

Invitation to the Lord's Supper

Hymn

Prayer of approach, and/or sharing of the peace

Reception into membership

  Questions to the newly baptized and church members

  Right hand of fellowship

  Laying on of hands

  Communion

  Hymn

  Benediction

Second Pattern

Baptismal Service

    Call to worship
    Hymn
    Prayer
    Reading
    Testimony
    Psalm
    Baptism   Introduction
                  Prayer
                  Questions to the candidate(s)
                  Baptism

     leader and newly baptized leave to change

    Hymn
    Prayer
    Offering

     leader and newly baptized return

    Reading
    Sermon—a charge to the baptized
    Hymn
    Laying on of hands
    Prayer
    Hymn
    Benediction

At a subsequent Communion Service

After praise and preaching, when the congregation is gathered at the Table for the Lord's Supper, the newly baptized are received into membership.

Baptism

The act of baptism may be placed as a climax to worship, following the reading and proclamation of the Gospel (to which baptism is of course the response), or it may come earlier, after opening worship and praise (in which case the sermon may more naturally become a charge to the newly baptized). It is customary for those being baptized to share in the preparation of the service, often by choosing hymns or songs.

It is right that those being baptized should tell their stories. People at the beginning of their Christian life will seldom find it easy or natural to speak to an entire congregation and must be helped to find a means of sharing with the congregation, so that this will not be an ordeal and will permit something of their joy to be communicated. Possibilities include extempore or prepared testimony, the introduction of a song or poem of special significance, an interview, or the circulation of written accounts before the service. The way in which the candidates share their faith will help to determine the place it occupies within the service, but it should obviously take place before their baptism.

More than one person may take part in the act of baptizing, to give a fuller expression of the involvement of the whole church community or simply to provide physical assistance.

Candidates for baptism may be invited to choose a member of the church to sit with them before the baptism, and to be waiting for them as they leave the baptistry, with a towel to dry their faces, and to help them up the steps.

Baptism is normally by total immersion, but alternative forms may be preferred because of illness or disability. Water from the baptistry may be poured over the person's head, which may be done while the person is within the baptistry, perhaps having been lowered into the water in a chair. The most appropriate means for the person concerned should be used, and informed medical advice should be sought and followed where necessary. Whatever the mode of baptism, the fact that it is believers' baptism must be clearly expressed and understood. In cases of mental handicap, care must be taken to find a means by which the candidate can appropriately make a declaration of faith.

Introduction

Because baptism is a unique event in the life of a Christian and may be new to many members of the congregation, explanation and teaching will be an important part of the service. Suggested readings include: Isaiah 6: 1–9a; Matthew 3: 1–12; 3: 13–17; Mark 1: 1–13; John 3: 1–8; Acts 2: 38–42; 8: 26–39; 9: 1–19; 10: 34–48; 16: 11–15; 16: 25–34; 19: 1–7; Romans 6: 3–11; Ephesians 4: 1–6; Colossians 3: 1–17; 1 Timothy 6: 12; Titus 3: 3–7; Hebrews 10: 19–25.

The following statement might be used as an introduction to baptism, or as the basis for teaching or preaching.

On the day of Pentecost, the Apostle Peter proclaimed the good news of God and called his hearers to repent and be baptized in the name of Jesus Christ. Following in that tradition, we baptize those whom Jesus Christ has led to repentance and new life in faith.

Jesus was baptized in the river Jordan by John. In baptism, believers take their stand in union with him, and declare their faith in his death and resurrection. Their baptism marks an ending and a beginning in life: they are washed free of sin to begin a new life in the power and joy of the Spirit. The public confession of faith in Christ is also an act of obedience to God, and the means of entry into his Church.

Baptism is our response to all that God has done for us in Christ, and a celebration of all that he gives of himself in his Spirit. The initiative is God's, and in baptism his grace is displayed.

Baptized into union with him, you have all put on Christ like a garment.   *Galatians 3: 27*

> *Or the following may be used (and adapted if only one person is to be baptized):*

My friends, you have heard —— tell of the pilgrimages of faith that *have* brought *them* to this point today. *They are* here because in Jesus Christ *they have* found a living Lord. *They have* met him in a personal way, and *know* that Jesus, the Son of God, loves *them*, and that he gave himself to die for *them* on a cross. *Each* knows that Jesus, the Son of God, was not defeated by death but was raised to life, and calls us to accept his forgiveness and hope, and to share in his resurrection life.

In baptism *they express* this belief, consecrating *themselves* in a special way to commitment and service. *They* will enter the water in obedience, believing that baptism is commanded by Christ himself. As *they go* under the water and *rise* from it, *they give* witness to *their* desire to die to self and rise with Christ to new life.

They come surrounded by the love and prayers of this church family and upheld by the great continuous prayer that unites us with the universal Church of Christ in heaven and on earth.

They come as much loved children of a Father who welcomes *them* here. Jesus is *their* brother, and *they are* bound to him by his Holy Spirit. God is glad, and we are glad, that *they have* come. This is a special moment—let us pray for *them*.

Prayer

Almighty God, we give you thanks that at the beginning your Spirit moved upon the face of the waters and you said, 'Let there be light'. We give you thanks that you led your people through the water of the Red Sea, out of slavery, and into the freedom of the Promised Land.

We give you thanks for your Son, Jesus Christ, who was baptized in the river Jordan. We thank you that he passed through the deep waters of his death on the cross and was raised to life in triumph. Send your Holy Spirit that this baptism may be for your servants a union with Christ in his death and resurrection that, as Christ was raised from death through the glory of the Father, *they* also might live new *lives*. Send your Holy

Spirit anew upon *them* that *they* may be brought into the fellowship of the Body of Christ and may grow in Christ's likeness.

> *Or:*

Lord God, you know each one of us better than we know ourselves. In your Son you have shown us love that is greater than we can ever appreciate. In your Spirit we are bound closer to you and to each other.

We pray especially for your servants ——. We ask that *they* may know the fullness of your love and the filling of your Spirit as in baptism *they signify their* desire to follow your Son.

May this important step on *their lives' journeys* wash away the fears and sins of the past. May all *they know* of you be enhanced and magnified, and may what happens today underline *their* progress towards a future of sure and certain hope.

This we ask through Jesus Christ our Lord.

Declaration of Faith

> *This is an integral part of the act of worship and it is important that the congregation can hear what is happening. It is good to be in or near the baptistry at this point.*

LEADER —— do you believe in one God, Father, Son, and Holy Spirit?

CANDIDATE I do.

LEADER In obedience to the call of our risen Lord Jesus Christ, do you repent of your sins and come to be baptized?

CANDIDATE	I do.
LEADER	With the help of the Holy Spirit, do you offer your life in service to God wherever he may call you to go?
CANDIDATE	I do.
LEADER	Then come and be baptized.

Or:

LEADER	Do you confess Jesus Christ as your Lord and Saviour?
CANDIDATE	I do.
LEADER	Do you turn from sin, renounce evil, and intend to follow Christ?
CANDIDATE	I do.
LEADER	Will you seek to live within the fellowship of his Church, and to serve him in the world?
CANDIDATE	With the Lord's help, I will.

Immediately before baptism, the candidate(s) may be given a text chosen for them by their minister.

The Baptism

Each candidate then enters the baptistry, to be baptized with the following words:

Having heard of your repentance and your faith, I now baptize you, —— my *brother/sister*, in the name of God the Father, God the Son, and God the Holy Spirit.

Or:

——, on your profession of faith and pledge of

allegiance I gladly baptize you in the name of the Father, the Son, and the Holy Spirit.

As they emerge from the water the candidates may align themselves with the Church through the ages by making aloud the profession of faith:

CANDIDATE   Jesus is Lord!

CONGREGATION   Hallelujah!

Baptism may be followed by the singing of a hymn. If there are a number of candidates, a verse may be sung between each baptism.
During the period when the baptized and baptizer(s) are changing, prayers may be offered, a solo may be sung, or the congregation may be led in praise to emphasize the Gospel call.
It may be helpful to end this period by collecting the congregation's offering. This can then be brought forward when the leader and baptized return.

Words of Appeal

The challenge and witness of baptism may be followed by inviting others to respond to the Gospel.

The Laying on of Hands

Like baptism, the laying on of hands requires some explanation. Appropriate readings and verses are: Acts 8: 14–17; 9: 17–19; 13: 1–3; 19: 1–6; 1 Timothy 4: 14; Revelation 1: 17.

The New Testament records that those who were

baptized often received the laying on of hands as a sign of commissioning for service.

We are now to lay hands on —, who *have* been baptized, as a sign of blessing and an act of commissioning, and to ask that *they* may be fully equipped for *their* vocation as *servants* of Jesus Christ in the Church and in the world.

The candidate(s) may be addressed with words of scripture:

You are a chosen race, a royal priesthood, a dedicated nation, a people claimed by God for his own, to proclaim the glorious deeds of him who has called you out of darkness into his marvellous light.

1 Peter 2: 9

You are light for all the world. You must shed light among your fellows, so that, when they see the good you do, they may give praise to your Father in heaven.

Matthew 5: 14a, 16

Each candidate kneels and the leader(s) lay(s) hands on each, offering prayer such as:

Lord, bless *these* your servants and strengthen *them* by your Holy Spirit as we commission *them* for service in the Church and the world in the name of the Lord Jesus Christ.

The candidate(s) stand(s) as the leader says:

You are no longer aliens in a foreign land, but fellow-citizens with God's people, members of God's household. You are built on the foundation of the apostles and prophets, with Christ Jesus himself as the cornerstone. *Ephesians 2: 19–20*

Reception into Membership

New Members may be received after baptism, or when membership is transferred from another church, or on profession of faith. Reception into membership takes place when the congregation is gathered around the Table immediately before the Lord's Supper. When reception follows baptism, the profession of faith will be unnecessary.

Introductory Statement

We are now to receive —— into the membership of —— Baptist Church. We enter into a covenant with *them* to share with each other in building up the Church to the glory of God, working alongside one another in his service in the world, and encouraging one another in the love of God.

Profession of Faith

LEADER ——, do you declare your faith in the One God, Father, Son, and Holy Spirit, having found new life in him?

CANDIDATE I do.

Questions to Candidate

LEADER ——, do you believe God has called you to serve Christ as part of this local Baptist church?

CANDIDATE	I do.
LEADER	Do you commit yourself to love and serve the Lord within this church community and in the world; and being filled with the Holy Spirit, to fulfil your ministry in the Body of Christ?
CANDIDATE	I do.

Or:

LEADER	——, do you believe that as a follower of Christ you are called to band together with other believers in his Church? Do you now believe that you are called to be part of this church community in ——, and do you accept the Baptist principles to which we give expression?
CANDIDATE	I do.
LEADER	Do you now commit yourself to love and to work, to share and to serve within this church community and within our world? Do you believe that here you may learn and grow and do you accept the responsibility of being a member of this church?
CANDIDATE	I do.

Response of Church

Inviting church members to stand, the leader asks them:

LEADER	Do you welcome —— into the family of God in this local church?
MEMBERS	We do.

LEADER	Do you promise to love, encourage, strengthen, guide, pray for, and care for — as an equal partner in the Body of Christ?
MEMBERS	We do.
	Or:
LEADER	Do you commit yourselves to receive — as a member of this church, offering to *him/her* your friendship and love?
MEMBERS	We do.
LEADER	Do you receive — as a *brother/sister* in Christ, being ready to hear and serve the Lord in *him/her*, and to serve the Lord with *him/her*?
MEMBERS	We do.

Reception into Membership

Offering the hand of fellowship to the new member(s), the leader says, for example:

In the name of the Lord Jesus Christ, and on behalf of this fellowship, I welcome you into our membership.

The new member(s) may be invited to sign the church roll.

Prayer *such as:*

Lord our God, you have joined us together in Christ, and from each to the other you will speak your Word of comfort and challenge. Make us ready to listen and swift to act, both church and new member(s). May *they* not fail you, nor we fail *them*.

Or:

Lord God, we praise you for the ways you guide our lives and give sense and purpose to them, and thank you for all the direction and purpose that you have given in the lives of ——. We are grateful that in this church *they have* found a home. We pray that the sense of your direction and purpose may not leave *them* but may grow and mature and bear fruit in *their lives* and the life of the church. Send your blessing on our life together; through Jesus Christ our Lord.

The service continues with the Lord's Supper.

INFANT PRESENTATION

The form and content of a service of presentation will vary considerably not only from one church to another but also from one service to another. There is variety in the understanding of infant presentation and the circumstances of the family involved.

In this material it has been assumed that some of the following will be understood to be happening: that we thank God for the birth of a child; that the parents will dedicate themselves to the Christian upbringing of the child, and the church will commit itself to support them; that a child is being presented to, and received by, the congregation in token of God's loving acknowledgement of the child; and that this may be further symbolized by the naming of the child.

The circumstances of the family involved can vary in many ways: the child may no longer be an infant; one parent may be absent from the service or indeed from the home; the parents may be unmarried; the child may be disabled; the service may be taking place after adoption; there may be little or no church connection. These circumstances will have to be taken into account with pastoral sensitivity and careful judgement in each case.

Two patterns are given, either of which would normally form part of Sunday worship, taking place when all ages are present. The first order is appropriate when the parents are able to make a full commitment to a Christian upbringing of their child within the life of the church. The second order asks for a less explicitly Christian commitment, which might sometimes be more realistic.

It should be noted that in a Baptist church, the naming of a child has no legal significance.

First Pattern

The Presentation of Infants

Introduction

In the name of Jesus Christ, we welcome today —— , with their new *son/daughter*, and members of their wider families.

(*Parents' names*) —— are here to present their child before the Lord, as Jesus was presented in the Temple by his parents. In so doing they recognize that their child is not their personal property but belongs also to God, and that as parents they have responsibilities before God. In their promises they will commit themselves to fulfil those responsibilities.

As a church, we shall welcome their child into our family, as Jesus welcomed children brought to him.

Also we shall promise in the presence of God to offer our support and friendship to this child and *his/her* family, and to join with *his/her* parents in sharing our faith in Jesus Christ in the hope that *he/she* may one day discover such a faith for *himself/herself*.

Finally we shall ask God for his blessing on his child.

Let us begin by recalling the promises and commands of God concerning children.

Readings

Hear, Israel: the Lord is our God, the Lord our one God; and you must love the Lord your God with all your heart, and with all your soul, and with all your strength. These commandments which I give you this day are to be remembered and taken to heart; repeat them to your children, and speak of them both indoors and out of doors, when you lie down and when you get up.
Deuteronomy 6: 4–7

Jesus said, 'Truly I tell you: unless you turn round and become like children, you will never enter the kingdom of Heaven. Whoever humbles himself and becomes like this child will be greatest in the kingdom of Heaven.'
Matthew 18: 3–4

They brought children for him to touch. The disciples rebuked them, but when Jesus saw it he was indignant, and said to them, 'Let the children come to me; do not try to stop them; for the kingdom of God belongs to such as these. Truly I tell you: whoever does not accept the kingdom of God like a child will never enter it.' And he put his arms round them, laid his hands on them, and blessed them.
Mark 10: 13–16

Also Matthew 18: 1–5; 18: 10–14; Luke 2: 22–32, 39–40; 18: 15–17. Responsive readings and prayers may be found in **Baptist Praise and Worship.**

Prayers of Thanksgiving

A prayer of praise and thanksgiving for God as creator of all life, and for the gift of this child's life in particular, such as:

Lord God, we praise you, the creator of all things,
the giver of all life, and the Father of each person.
Joyfully we thank you for the gift of new life
in the birth of this child.
For all that you have given and will give to us
through *him/her*;
for the potential of *his/her* new life;
for the love and hope *he/she* has awakened;
and for the care which surrounds *him/her*;
accept our thanks and praise;
in the name of Jesus Christ.

Promises

The parents are invited to stand, and are asked by the minister or leader:

LEADER	——, do you thank God for his gift of your child, and do you accept the joys and duties of parenthood, promising to give love and care to your child?
PARENTS	We do.
LEADER	Do you promise to bring your *son/daughter* up within the Christian community and to share your own faith with *him/her*?
PARENTS	We do.
LEADER	What names have you given to your *son/daughter*?
PARENTS	——.

Taking the child from the mother and going to the front or centre of the church, the leader says:

——, we welcome you in the name of the Lord.

And having invited the congregation to answer 'We do', asks them:

LEADER   Do you promise to offer to —— and *his/her* family your love and care, and to join with *his/her* parents in sharing our Christian faith?

CONGREGATION   We do.

Blessing

Placing his or her hand on the child's head, the leader says:

——, the Lord bless you and keep you;
the Lord make his face to shine upon you
and be gracious unto you;
the Lord lift up the light of his countenance upon
you and give you peace.   *Numbers 6: 24–26*

Leader returns child to father

Prayer

A prayer should be offered for the future of the child and the family, such as:

Loving God, we pray for this child and *his/her* family.
May they know the challenge and comfort of your love, and see its power.
Take all that we offer to ——, our care, our wisdom,

and our mistakes, and through them reveal yourself.
Take the experiences which —— will have, and through
them speak your gracious Word.
As —— grows in body, mind, and spirit, feed and guide
him/her by your Spirit, bring *him/her* safe through
childhood and youth, and lead *him/her* to make the
good confession that 'Jesus Christ is Lord';
Through Christ your Son, our Saviour.

> *The church's care and continued support may be
> symbolized in the presentation of a certificate, a
> bible, or another gift. The parents may entrust the
> child to the care of the crèche or nursery
> department.*

Second Pattern

The Blessing of Infants

Introduction

In the name of Jesus Christ we welcome —— and their baby ——.

Because all life is a gift from God, we shall thank him for his gift of this child, and we shall ask —— to declare their intention to bring up their child with love and care.

Finally we shall ask God to bless —— and we shall pray for *his/her* future.

Readings

Matthew 18: 1–4; 18: 10–14; Mark 10: 13–16; Luke 18: 15–17.

Prayer of Thanksgiving

God our Father, maker of all that is living,
we praise you for the wonder and joy of creation.
We thank you for the love that has summoned this child into being,
for a safe delivery, and for the privilege of parenthood.
Accept our thanks and praise; through Jesus Christ our Lord.

The Promise

The minister asks the parents:

LEADER   By bringing —— to the Lord, do you recognize your responsibilities as parents to love and care for *him/her*, and do you promise to try by your example to teach *him/her* a good and true way of life?

PARENTS   We do.

Blessing

The mother gives the child to the minister who, placing his or her hand on the child's head, says:

——, you are one of God's children, held forever in his love. The blessing of God, Father, Son, and Holy Spirit, rest and remain with you now and always.

Or:

——, may the Lord bless you and take care of you;
May the Lord be kind and gracious to you;
May the Lord look on you with favour and give you peace.   *Numbers 6: 24–26*

The minister returns the child to the father

Prayer for the Family's Future

Heavenly Father, bless the home of this child, and help all the family to live together in your love. Help them to serve you and each other, and to be always ready to show your love to those in need; for the sake of Jesus Christ our Lord.

Alternative material and notes

Other readings which might be considered include Psalms 8 and 127, and Ephesians 6: 1–4.

Parents' promises need not be in the question and answer form in the services, but could be read aloud.

In the case of handicapped children the following prayer might be used or adapted:

Loving God, your Son Jesus called on his friends to join with him in giving honour to children, not for what they might become but for what they are: those to whom your Kingdom belongs.

As we greet this child today, we do so conscious not only of how *his/her* disability may affect the future we want for *him/her*, but also conscious of all that *he/she* already is.

Help us to honour this child in *his/her* own right, as an example to all who would enter your Kingdom;
and to welcome this child with love, knowing that to receive *him/her* in your name is to receive you.

As the family face the challenges of the future, may all their happiness and sorrow be filled with the joy of finding in one another your gift of yourself; through Jesus Christ our Lord.

In the case of adoption, the wording of the services will need careful attention. References to the birth of the child might be replaced by referring to the life of the child.

CHRISTIAN MARRIAGE

Planning a wedding service with an engaged couple can be an important part of the pastoral care offered in preparation for marriage, and there is considerable freedom of choice to exercise and enjoy. However, there are a number of legal requirements that a wedding service in a nonconformist church must fulfil.

1. The church must be registered for marriages.

2. The marriage service itself must be held between 8.00 a.m. and 6.00 p.m.

3. The doors must be not so closed as to prevent people from entering.

4. An Authorized Person or Registrar must be present to witness and register the marriage. The Authorized Person need not be (perhaps preferably not) the person conducting the service.

5. There must be at least two people present (apart from the Authorized Person or Registrar) who are able to act as witnesses.

6. The couple must each make a declaration of no impediment as follows:

   > I do solemnly declare that I know not
   > of any lawful impediment why I ——
   > may not be joined in matrimony to ——.

7. The couple's vows must include the following words if a Registrar is present to register the marriage:

> I call upon these persons here present
> to witness that I, ——,
> do take thee, ——,
> to be my lawful wedded *wife/husband*.

If an Authorized Person is present to register the marriage the following alternative words may be used:

> I, ——, do take thee, ——,
> to be my wedded *wife/husband*.

In these legal forms of words, the names used should be the full names, including surnames, which the parties use and by which they are generally known. If these names are different from the names given on the certificate(s), this difference must be cleared by the Authorized Person or Registrar prior to the marriage taking place.

Details of registration and the necessary certificate(s) are not given here as they belong to the responsibility of the Authorized Person or Registrar.

There are special provisions to enable marriages to take place in the homes of those who are housebound, for marriages for those who are detained, and how deaf and dumb persons are to make their declarations and vows. For these matters the advice of the Authorized Person or Registrar should be sought.

The law concerning marriage is subject to change, and at the time of writing a revision is anticipated. It is most important that those conducting wedding services should be aware of, and comply with, the requirements of the law currently in force.

There are various customs attached to the wedding service which need not be followed and may well be questioned in the light of contemporary views of marriage. For example, the custom of the bride arriving after the bridegroom may be varied by both the man and woman entering the church at the beginning of the service and walking down either side to meet at the front. The custom of the bride being given away by her father may be omitted, repeated for the groom, or extended by including other members of the couple's families and the whole congregation. Alternatives are offered in the following material.

It is suggested that the couple do not repeat their vows after the minister, but read them from previously prepared cards.

Since marriages are very different in character, depending on the age and circumstances of the man and woman, it is important that, before use, the following material is carefully examined for any inappropriateness to the wedding taking place.

The elements of the wedding ceremony within the marriage service—introduction, declaration of no impediment, question of intent, 'giving away', vows, giving of ring(s), declaration of marriage, and prayer and blessing—are placed together as the climax of the service in the suggested order. Other orders are possible, and the following is an alternative.

Entrance of bride or couple

Call to worship

Hymn

Introduction

Declaration of no impediment,
   question of intent,
   and giving away

Prayer

Vows, giving of ring(s),
    declaration of marriage

Hymn or song

Reading

Sermon

Prayer and blessing

Hymn

Signing of register

Wedding procession

Christian Marriage

Welcome

*Having met the bride and bridal party at the
door, the minister goes to the front of the church
and says:*

On behalf of —— *(name of church)*, I welcome you all
to this service to celebrate the Christian marriage of
—— and ——.

Would you please stand for the entry of the bride.

Call to Worship

Hymn

Prayer

A prayer of approach should be offered, such as:

God of love, we praise you.
You made the world in love, giving us freedom;

in Christ you lived by love, accepting all its hurt and
sharing all its healing;
by your Spirit you are present in love, everywhere and
always, here and now.
As we respond to your great love,
accept the worship and commitment we all bring,
and bless the commitment of —— and ——.
Let the love of Christ be present in everything done and
begun today; through Jesus Christ our Lord.

> *Prayers for the couple may be offered now or
> before the vows, such as:*

Father, hear our prayers for —— and —— who, with
faith in you and in each other, pledge their love today.
May they be as aware of your presence as they are of
ours, and confident that you are able to help them fulfil
their promises in their life together; through Jesus
Christ our Lord.

Living God, you have commanded us to love each
other.
We thank you now for the love which grows between a
man and a woman, which has brought these two
together here to declare themselves one before you and
their families and friends.
As they make their promises to each other, may they
do so humbly and penitently [and in the confidence
that you will forgive all their failures of the past].
May they begin their life together with your own love
in heart and mind, and may we all continue, all our
lives, to walk with you and glorify your name; through
Jesus Christ our Lord.

> *See also prayers in* **Baptist Praise and Worship.**

Reading

Such as: Genesis 1: 26–28, 31a; 2: 4b–8, 18–24;
Psalms 33: 2–9; 145: 8–10, 15, 17–18; Song of
Solomon 2: 8–10, 14, 16 and 8: 6–7; Jeremiah 31;
31–34; Matthew 5: 13–16; Mark 10: 6–9; John 2:
1–11; 1 Conrinthians 13; Ephesians 3: 14–21; 5:
21–33; Colossians 3: 12–17; 1 John 4: 7–12.

Sermon

Hymn

After which the couple and attendants should
remain standing.

Declaration of Purpose

The minister or leader shall say:

We are here to witness the marriage of —— and ——.

The Bible says that God has made us in his image, male
and female. We are separate and different yet able, in
love, to meet, know, and delight in one another. In
Christian marriage two people trusting in this mystery
of love commit themselves to live faithfully together for
life, in plenty or need, joy or sorrow.
For this purpose —— and —— are here today. They will
give themselves to one another so that God's gift of
love may join them together as husband and wife.

It is our privilege not only to witness this, but to
celebrate it with them, and to acknowledge their
marriage ourselves.

In marriage wife and husband belong to one another
and begin a new life together in the community. We
shall offer them our support.

All this we do before God the source of life and love. All who trust their lives to one another are relying on the power of love and the faithfulness of God, so we shall ask God to send his blessing on —— and —— that their new life together may be filled with joy, may bring them ever closer to one another, and may make them ever more open to God whose love gives meaning to theirs.

This is the way of life, which —— and —— are now about to begin. Anyone who can show any reason why they may not lawfully be married should say so now.

Or:

We have come together in the presence of God, to witness the marriage of —— and ——,
to ask his blessing on them, and to share in their joy. Jesus Christ was himself a guest at a wedding in Cana of Galiee, and through his Spirit he is with us now.

God has made us male and female, and marriage is his gift, a holy mystery in which man and woman become one flesh, united in love, and called to be faithful to each other throughout their lives.

Marriage is given so that husband and wife may comfort and help each other, living faithfully together in need and in plenty, in sorrow and in joy. It is given that with delight and tenderness they may know each other in love, and, through the joy of their bodily union, may strengthen the union of their hearts and lives. It is given so that the stability it imparts to their relationship may be a source of strength to others [and the foundation of a secure family life for any children they may have].

In marriage husband and wife belong to one another,
and they begin a new life in the community. It is a way
of life that all should honour; it must not be
undertaken carelessly, lightly, or selfishly, but
reverently, responsibly, and after serious thought.
This is the way of life, created and hallowed by God,
that —— and —— are now about to enter. Therefore
anyone who can show any reason why they may not
lawfully be married should say so now.

Declaration of No Impediment

The minister turns to the couple and says:

If either of you know of any reason why you may not
lawfully marry, you should say so now.

*The minister invites the man to say after him/her
or the man says:*

I do solemnly declare
that I know not
of any lawful impediment
why I, ——,
may not be joined in matrimony
to ——.

Similarly, the woman repeats or says:

I do solemnly declare
that I know not
of any lawful impediment
why I, ——,
may not be joined in matrimony
to ——.

Question of Intent

LEADER ——, will you take —— as your wife in Christian marriage? Will you love her, comfort her, honour, and keep her, in sickness and in health, and be faithful to her as long as you both live?

GROOM I will.

LEADER ——, will you take —— as your husband in Christian marriage? Will you love him, comfort him, honour, and keep him, in sickness and in health, and be faithful to him as long as you both live?

BRIDE I will.

With rephrasing this question could be asked to both together.

The Giving Away

Here the minister may ask:

Who gives this woman to be married to this man?

FATHER I do.

Or:

My wife and I do.

Or, inviting first the families (or parents), and then the congregation to stand, the minister may ask:

Do you, the families of —— and ——, give your love and blessing to this new family?

PARENTS OR FAMILIES We do.

LEADER Will all of you, by God's grace, do everything in your power to uphold and care for these two in their life together?

CONGREGATION We will.

All sit. The minister invites the couple to turn and face one another, join their hands, and make the following promises.

The minister invites the man to say after him/her or the man says:

I, ——, do take thee, ——, to be my wedded wife, to have and to hold, from this day forward, for better for worse, for richer for poorer, in sickness and in health, to love and to cherish, until we are parted by death, and to this end I give you my word.

Similarly the woman repeats or says:

I, ——, do take thee, ——, to be my wedded husband, to have and to hold, from this day forward, for better for worse, for richer for poorer, in sickness and in health, to love and to cherish, until we are parted by death, and to this end I give you my word.

If the Registrar is present to register the marriage, the vows should commence with these words:

I call upon these persons here present
to witness that I ——
do take thee ——
to be my lawful wedded *wife/husband*

The Giving of the Ring(s)

The following form of words may be used at the exchange of rings:

I give you this ring as a sign of our marriage.
With my body I honour you, all that I am I give to
you, and all that I have I share with you within the
love of God, Father, Son, and Holy Spirit.

> *Or:*

I give you this ring in God's name, as a symbol of all
that we shall share.

> *If there is only one ring, the woman may respond
> 'I receive this ring . . .'.*

Declaration of Marriage

Since —— and —— have declared in the presence of
God and this congregation that they will live together
in Christian marriage, since they have made their
promises to each other, and symbolized their marriage
by joining hands, and by giving and receiving a ring (*or*
rings), I therefore pronounce them husband and wife in
the name of the Father, the Son, and the Holy Spirit.
Those whom God has joined together, let no one
separate.

Prayer and Blessing

> *A prayer (for which the couple may wish to
> kneel) such as:*

Eternal God, Creator and Father of us all, we praise
you for creating humanity male and female, so that
each may find fulfilment in the other.

We praise you for the ways in which love comes into
our lives, and for all the joys that can come to men and
women through marriage.

Today, we thank you for —— and ——, for your gift to them of life, and for bringing them together in marriage.

We thank you for the love and care of their parents, which has guided them to maturity and prepared them for each other. We thank you for their commitment to one another and to a life planted in love and built on love. With them we pray for their parents, that at this moment of parting they may find new happiness as they share their children's joy.

Help —— and —— to keep the promises they have made, to be loyal and faithful to each other, and to support one another throughout their life together; may they bear each other's burdens and share each other's joys.

Help them to be honest and patient with each other, to be loving and wise parents of any children they have, and to make their home a place of welcome and peace.

In their future together, may they enjoy each other's lives and grow through each other's love; through Jesus Christ our Lord.

> *The blessing may be said by the whole congregation and/or accompanied by the laying on of hands.*

—— and ——, the Lord bless you and keep you;
the Lord make his face to shine upon you and be gracious to you;
the Lord lift up the light of his countenance upon you and give you peace. *Numbers 6: 24–26*

Hymn

Benediction

Signing of the Register

*The minister, the couple, the best man and bridesmaids,
the couple's parents and any others required to act as
witnesses, now leave the church in order to sign the
registers.*

*At this point it is traditional for an organ voluntary
to be played, or a solo to be sung. Alternatively, the
congregation could be led in prayer and praise. When
the signing is completed, the couple lead the
congregation from the church.*

Additional Material

*Various forms of the vows are possible, and there is no
reason why a couple should not compose their own,
providing of course that they contain the legal form of
words required. Some of the alternatives are:*

In the presence of God and this community,
**I, ——, do take thee, ——, to be my wedded
wife/husband;**

> *or where a Registrar is present to register the
> marriage:*

**I call upon these persons here present to witness that I,
——, do take thee, ——, to be my lawful wedded
wife/husband,**

to have and to hold from this day forward,
in joy and in sorrow,
in plenty and in want,
in sickness and in health,

to love and to cherish,
as long as we both shall live.
This is my solemn vow.

> *Both groom and bride having said one of the legal
> forms of words, they join hands and say:*

GROOM ——, I will love you in good times and bad.
I will love you when it is easy and when it is not.
I will love you when love brings us close, and when
love pushes us apart. I will love you when my love is
obvious and when it is hidden by my faults. Please go
on trusting me.

BRIDE ——, I will go on trusting you and loving you in
good times and bad. I will love you when it is easy and
when it is not. I will love you when love brings us
close, and when love pushes us apart. I will love you
when my love is obvious and when it is hidden by my
faults. Please go on trusting me.

GROOM I will. Rich or poor, well or ill, strong or
weak: I will, till death parts us. It is God's intention. I
give my word.

BRIDE Rich or poor, well or ill, strong or weak: I will,
till death parts us. It is God's intention. I give my
word.

> *These vows with their emphasis on the
> continuance of the relationship might be
> appropriate for services for the blessing of a
> marriage. In such cases, the question of intent
> might be modified by substituting the words:*

LEADER ——, do you acknowledge —— to be your
wife/husband in Christian marriage? Do you
promise to continue to love her . . . (etc.).

GROOM/BRIDE I do.

If it was wished to use one of the legal forms of words, they could be adapted similarly:

I (call upon these persons here present to witness that I), ——, have taken thee, ——, to be ....

Alternative prayer and blessing:

Lord God, Heavenly Father, in your great love you created us male and female and made the union of husband and wife an image of the covenant between you and your people.

Send your Holy Spirit to pour out your blessing on —— and —— who have this day given themselves to each other in marriage.

Bless them in their work and in their companionship;
in their sleeping and in their waking;
in their joys and in their sorrows;
in their life and in their death.

Let their love for each other be a seal upon their hearts, a mantle about their shoulders, and a crown upon their heads.

Bless them so that all may see, in their lives together in the community of your people, a vision of your Kingdom on earth.

And finally, in the fullness of time, welcome them into the glory of your presence; through your Son Jesus Christ.

A responsive blessing:

May God, the Father, give you his joy.
COUPLE Amen.

May the Son of God guide and help you in good times and bad.

COUPLE Amen.

May the Holy Spirit always fill your hearts with his love.

COUPLE Amen.

May almighty God bless you, the Father, the Son, and the Holy Spirit.

COUPLE Amen.

THE FUNERAL

A Service of Hope

The form and content of funeral services will reflect the variety of pastoral needs. Pastoral concerns should always be uppermost, and it is hoped that the material offered here can be adapted for use in a variety of situations, including those where the minister feels that the person who has died has shown no discernible Christian faith. This section includes two basic patterns.

The first provides a service of committal followed by a thanksgiving service. The committal will usually be an intimate service for the family and close friends and may well, for practical reasons, take place in a crematorium or cemetery chapel. The thanksgiving service will normally take place in a church building and will reflect the pattern of worship familiar to the local congregation.

The second pattern is the more traditional order of readings and prayers followed by the act of committal. This may mean the whole service taking place at a crematorium or cemetery chapel, or the major part in the church building and the act of committal at the appropriate place.

Local arrangements or different cultural traditions should be confirmed with the undertaker or attendant.

After material for the burial or scattering of ashes, the section concludes with additional material for circumstances of particular pastoral need.

Suggested readings: Psalms 8; 16; 23; 27; 30; 42: 1–8;
43: 3–5; 46; 90; 103; 116; 118: 14–21, 28–29; 121;
130; 138; 139: 1–14, 17–18, 23; John 5: 19–25; 6:
35–40; 11: 17–27; Romans 8: 18, 28, 35, 37–39;
1 Corinthians 15: 1–4, 20–26, 35–38, 42–44, 50, 53–
58; 2 Corinthians 4: 7–18; 4: 16–5: 18; Philippians 3:
10–21; 1 Thessalonians 4: 13–18; 1 Peter 1: 3–9;
Revelation 7: 9–17.

First Pattern

(Funeral service with committal followed later by a
service of thanksgiving.)

Funeral Service with Committal

The committal should provide an opportunity for
'letting go' of the person who has died and also be an
occasion for ministering to the needs of those left
behind. If it precedes the thanksgiving service, it may
include prayers asking for strength to help the
mourners through the difficulties of the more public
event.

Welcome

We have come here to say farewell to ——, to thank
God for *his/her* life and to commit *him/her* and
ourselves into God's loving care.

Listen now to the promises of Scripture: draw strength
and comfort from them, that you might face this hour
trusting in the love and faithfulness of God.

Sentences

The steadfast love of the Lord never ceases, his compassion never fails; every morning they are renewed.

Lamentations 3: 22–23

Blessed are those who mourn for they shall be comforted.

Matthew 5: 4

'As a mother comforts her child so I will comfort you,' says the Lord.

Isaiah 66: 13

Praise be to the God and Father of our Lord Jesus Christ who in his mercy gave us new birth into a living hope through the resurrection of Jesus Christ from the dead! The inheritance to which we are born is one that nothing can destroy or spoil or wither.

1 Peter 1: 3–4

I am convinced that there is nothing in death or life, in the realms of spirits or superhuman powers, in the world as it is or the world as it shall be, in the forces of the universe, in heights or depths—nothing in all creation that can separate us from the love of God in Christ Jesus our Lord.

Romans 8: 38–39

Prayer *expressing trust and asking for strength and assurance may be offered extempore or as follows:*

Heavenly Father, in your Son Jesus Christ you have given us a true faith and a sure hope. Strengthen this faith and hope in us all our days, that we may live as those who believe in the communion of saints, the forgiveness of sins and the resurrection to eternal life; through Jesus Christ our Lord.

Eternal God, the Lord of life, the conqueror of death,
our help in every time of trouble, comfort us who
mourn. Give us grace, in the presence of death, to
worship you; and enable us to put our whole trust in
your goodness and mercy; through Jesus Christ our
Lord.

Loving God, we come to you in our need.
You have given us birth and now we face the mystery
of death. Help us to find you in the whole of life, its
beginning and its ending. Help us to discover you in
our pain as well as our joy, in our doubts as well as
our believing, that we might find comfort in your word
and light for our darkness.
In the name of Jesus we ask it.

>   *A hymn may now be sung, or a psalm read*
>   *together.*

Scripture Reading

Brief Address

Prayers, *extempore or otherwise, should now express thanks*
for all that God has done in Christ, and for the life of
the deceased, and should seek the comfort of God for
those who are bereaved.

>   *Thanksgiving for Victory in Christ:*

Eternal God, you are the creator, the giver of life and,
in Jesus Christ, you have given us a new life which
nothing can destroy.
In the resurrection of Jesus you have shown us that the
grave is not the end, but that your love holds us
through all things.
We thank and praise you for this hope, not based on

vain and wishful thinking, but on the message of Easter
and the life-giving power of your Spirit at work in your
people; through Jesus Christ, the life and hope of the
world.

Remembrance and Thanksgiving:

Loving God, we thank you for the gift of life.
Today we thank you for the life of —— and all that
he/she was. We thank you for memories which we can
keep, a source of comfort and continuing thankfulness.
Thank you for those aspects of *his/her* life which meant
so much to us; for ——.
By your grace, help us to commit —— into your hands.
Grant us your peace, for we ask it in the name of Jesus
Christ our Saviour.

*The Lord's Prayer may now be said, after which
the minister invites the congregation to stand.*

The Act of Committal

O Death, where is your victory? O Death, where is
your sting? Thanks be to God! He gives us victory
through our Lord Jesus Christ.

1 Corinthians 15: 55, 57

Words of committal such as:

Now that the earthly life of —— has come to an end,
we commit *his/her* body to be *cremated/buried*,
confident of the resurrection to eternal life; through our
Lord Jesus Christ.

Or:

Nothing can separate us from God's love, so we

commend —— into his hands. We commit the body of
our *sister/brother* to be *cremated/buried*, trusting in
God's mercy and compassion.

He will wipe every tear from their eyes. There shall be
an end to death, and to mourning and crying and pain,
for the old order has passed away.   *Revelation 21: 4*

> *After a brief silence there may follow prayers or
> reflections, such as:*

Now, Lord, let your servant go in peace:
your word has been fulfilled.
My own eyes have seen the salvation
which you have prepared in the sight of every people;
a light to reveal you to the nations
and the glory of your people Israel.

O Lord, support us all the day long of this troublous
life, until the shadows lengthen and the evening comes,
and the busy world is hushed, the fever of life is over
and our work done.
Then, Lord, in your mercy grant us safe lodging, a holy
rest, and peace at the last; through Jesus Christ our
Lord.

> *The service may end with a prayer, the words of
> the Grace, or a blessing, such as:*

God of peace, you brought back from the dead our
Lord Jesus, the great shepherd of the sheep, by the
blood of the eternal covenant.
Show us the peace we should seek;
show us the peace we should try to give;
show us the peace we may keep;

show us the peace you have given;
and make us what you want us to be;
through Jesus Christ, to whom be glory for ever.

Deep peace of the running wave to you,
deep peace of the flowing air to you,
deep peace of the quiet earth to you,
deep peace of the shining stars to you,
deep peace of the Son of peace to you.

A Service of Thanksgiving

*As this will take place either later in the same day as
the committal or at a later date, the mourners will take
their places in church in the same way as other
members of the congregation. This is a more public
event than the committal and, although there will be
prayers for the bereaved, the emphasis of the service
will be one of thanksgiving for what God has done in
Christ, for the life of the deceased, and prayers for
those things which the deceased believed to be
important. In the case of the death of a church
member, it may well be helpful for the prayers or other
parts of the service to be led by various members of the
fellowship. Materials from the other patterns in the
funeral section may be used here, as may material from
the general or Easter sections.*

Call to Worship

Hymn of Praise

Prayers of Praise and Confession *extempore or as follows:*

Loving and eternal God, we praise you.

Creator God, you have made the world in which we live and you have given us life. Merciful and compassionate Father, we praise and adore you.

Lord Jesus Christ, you have shown us the wonder and the cost of love through your life and through your death upon the cross. Risen Lord, we praise and adore you.

Life-giving Spirit, you renew and empower us to live as children of God and followers of Jesus. Spirit of love and hope, of joy and peace, we praise and adore you.

Creator God, forgive our squandering of life and its possibilities. We have missed opportunities for service and witness; we have misused and neglected gifts which you have entrusted to us. Forgive us.

Loving God, our love of you has been half-hearted and our love of others pitiful. You have shown us in Christ the glory of loving service. Forgive us.

Holy Spirit, we have lacked confidence in your power and assurance of your presence in our lives. Forgive us and fill us; for the sake of Jesus Christ our Saviour.

Assurance of Forgiveness

Here is a saying you must trust, one that merits full acceptance: 'Christ Jesus came into the world to save sinners.' Thanks be to God!

Scripture Reading

Sermon

The emphasis will be on thanksgiving for the person's life and on a triumphant proclamation of the resurrection hope.

Hymns or Song of Faith

Prayers

> *They may include thanksgiving for new life in Christ, for the life of the deceased, and for our own continuing lives, such as the following:*

Loving God, you have given us life with all its possibilities for growth and all its opportunities for service.

You have made us in your own image as men and women responsible and creative, open to great visions, and capable of great imagination.

In Jesus Christ you have shown us what, by your grace, we might be. When you raised him to life you showed us that death is not the end for those who put their trust in you.

Thank you for this new life in Christ and for the hope of its future fullness.

Now we thank you for the life of ——.

We thank you for all that *he/she* meant to us. We especially remember with gratitude . . .

We thank you for *his/her* faith in you and all that we saw of you through *him/her*.

As we remember, help us to commit ourselves anew to your service, so that our thanksgiving for —— might show itself in a readiness to be faithful to your will. This we pray in the name of Jesus Christ our Lord.

Hymn of Commitment

Dismissal and Blessing

May the love of the Lord Jesus draw us to himself;

may the power of the Lord Jesus strengthen us in his
service;
may the joy of the Lord Jesus fill our souls.

May the blessing of God almighty,
the Father, the Son, and the Holy Spirit,
be among you and remain with you always.

Second Pattern

(Funeral service ending with or followed by an act of committal.)

Funeral Service

Sentences

Jesus said, 'I am the resurrection and the life. Whoever believes in me will live, even though they die; and whoever lives and believes in me will never die.'

John 11: 25–26

The eternal God is your refuge, and underneath are the everlasting arms.

Deuteronomy 33: 27

God so loved the world that he gave his only Son, that whoever believes in him should not perish but have eternal life.

John 3: 16

The hour is coming, and now is, when the dead will hear the voice of the Son of God, and those who hear will live.

John 5: 25

At every turn life links us to the Lord, and when we die we come face to face with him. In life or death we are in the hands of the Lord. Christ lived and died and lives again to establish his lordship over dead and living.

Romans 14: 7–9

Things beyond our seeing, things beyond our hearing, things beyond our imagining, have all been prepared by God for those who love him.

1 Corinthians 2: 9

Welcome

> *A welcome may be given, in this form or another,
> which mentions the name of the deceased and
> acknowledges his or her death.*

We are here to honour —— who has died.
We are here because in one way or another this death
affects us all.
We are here to listen again to some of the great words
of the Christian faith; to consider, to remember, and in
quiet gratitude to give thanks for *his/her* life and our
own continuing lives.
We are here to renew our trust in God who has said: I
will not fail you or desert you.

Prayer *extempore or as follows:*

> Father, your love is stronger than death:
> by you we are all being brought to life.
> Help us, as we hear the promises of your Word, to
> believe them and to receive the comfort they offer.
> You are the giver of hope: fill us with joy and peace in
> believing, that our fears may be dispelled, our
> loneliness eased, and our hope re-awakened;
> through Jesus Christ our Lord.

Hymn or Song

Scripture Reading

Address

Prayers, *extempore or otherwise, should now express
thanksgiving for new life in Christ, and for the life of
the deceased, and should seek the comfort of God for
those who mourn. The general prayers below include*

each of these concerns, while the thematic prayers may be combined, or used as part of a larger extempore prayer.

General Prayers

Father God, we praise and thank you for the world in which we live and for the lives you have given us. We thank you for the new life offered to us in Jesus Christ, through his death on the cross and your raising him to life again.

We thank you for the life of —— and all that *he/she* meant to us; for those things in *his/her* life which gave us glimpses of your goodness and love. Especially we thank you for . . . .

Thank you that *his/her* sins are forgiven, all suffering is past and that your same love which now surrounds us also welcomes ——.

Help us to be content to release *him/her* to you, that our grief may neither be overwhelming nor unending. Assure us of your love, strengthen our trust in your grace, and grant us your peace; through Jesus Christ our Lord.

Our God, you are a Father to us:
you have given us life and cared for us. In Jesus Christ you have shown us that nothing can separate us from your love. Now, at a time when grief fills our hearts, help us to go on trusting your love.
We thank you for our lives and for the wonderful world that you have given us. Thank you for the life of ——: for . . . .

Now help us to let go; to trust your forgiveness and love. We know that you are with us in our grief. Ease

our loneliness, fill us with your peace, and help us to go on from today trusting you more fully.
We ask this in the name of Jesus Christ, the life of the world.

Thanksgiving for victory over death

Lord God, with your whole Church we offer you our thanks and praise for all you have done for humanity through Jesus Christ.
By giving him to live and die for us, you have disclosed your gracious plan for the world and shown that your love has no limit;
and by raising him from the dead, you have promised that those who trust in him will share his resurrection life.
For the assurance and hope of our faith, and for the saints whom you have received into your eternal joy, we thank you, heavenly Father.

Living God, we praise you for Jesus Christ who, for the joy that was in the future, went into the darkness of death so that we might continue to hope and rise above despair.
Thank you for his death, which has opened up the future for us;
thank you for his living among us now as risen Lord, leading us through death to undying life.
Keep convincing us that his resurrection means life for us, and that neither death, nor life, nor anything in all creation can deprive us of the future you are making for us.

Remembrance and Thanksgiving

Father God, we thank you for the life of ——, our

sister/brother, now gone from among us all; for all your goodness to *him/her* [through many days]; for all that *he/she* was to those who loved *him/her*, and for everything in *his/her* life that reflected your goodness and love.

And now we bless you that *his/her* sins are forgiven, all suffering and bitterness are past and forgotten.

Help us to be content to release *him/her* to you, our Father. In faith and hope we place *him/her* in your loving hands; through Jesus Christ our Lord.

God, source of life, beyond knowledge and thought, mysterious and profound:
we thank you because we have seen you in this *man/woman* who has died.

We thank you for your life in *him/her* with all its achievements, and for your love given and received by *him/her* among family and friends; for . . . *(thoughts appropriate to the life of the departed)*.

We thank you that *he/she* was such a person that our sorrow now is real and our loss great; one who enriched us by *his/her* presence.

Help us through *his/her* death to see more deeply into the meaning of *his/her* life and our own, and to grasp more firmly the hope that life is longer than our years and the love you have shown us in Christ is stronger than death; through that same Jesus Christ our Lord.

Loving God, we thank you for ——.
We thank you for the friendship *he/she* gave and for the strength and peace *he/she* brought; for the love *he/she* offered and received while with us on earth.

We pray that nothing good in this *man/woman's* life will be lost but will be of benefit to the world and that all that was important to *him/her* will be respected by those who follow. We ask that those of us who were close to *him/her* may now, because of *his/her* death, be close to one another and be aware of your love present through all things. We pray in the name of Jesus Christ our Lord.

For those who mourn

Almighty God, Father of all mercies and giver of all comfort: deal graciously, we pray, with those who mourn, that casting all their care on you, they may know the consolation of your love; through Jesus Christ our Lord.

O God of infinite compassion, look in love and pity on your sorrowing servants.
Be their support, their strength and their shield; that they may trust in you and be delivered out of their distresses; through Jesus Christ our Lord.

The Lord's Prayer and the following words of commendation may be used:

Depart, O Christian soul, out of this world,
in the name of God the Father almighty who created you,
in the name of Jesus Christ who redeemed you,
in the name of the Holy Spirit who sanctifies you.
May your rest be this day in peace and your dwelling in the paradise of God.

Merciful God, you have made us all and given your Son for our redemption. We commend our *sister/brother* —— to your perfect mercy and wisdom, for in you alone we put our trust.

> *When the committal is to be in another place, this part of the service may end with another hymn and an ascription of glory or the words of the grace.*

The God of all grace, who calls you to share his eternal glory in union with Christ, will himself perfect you and give you firmness, strength, and a sure foundation.
To him be the power for ever! Amen.   *1 Peter 5: 10–11*

And now may the grace of our Lord Jesus Christ, the love of God, and the fellowship of his Holy Spirit, be with us all, evermore.

The Committal

> *If the committal is in a different place from the funeral service, it may begin with a bible reading.*

Sentences

> The Lord says: 'Do not be afraid. I am the first and the last, and I am the living one: for I was dead and now I am alive for evermore.'   *Revelation 1: 17–18*

> We brought nothing into the world, and we cannot take anything out of the world. The Lord gave, and the Lord has taken away; blessed be the name of the Lord.
> *1 Timothy 6: 7; Job 1: 21*

Words of Committal

Seeing that the earthly life of our *sister/brother* has come to an end, we commit *his/her* body to be *buried/cremated*, earth to earth, ashes to ashes, dust to dust, confident of the resurrection to eternal life through our Lord Jesus Christ.

Or:

We have entrusted our *sister/brother* —— to God's merciful keeping, and we now commit *his/her* body *to the ground/to be cremated*: earth to earth, ashes to ashes, dust to dust, in sure and certain hope of the resurrection to eternal life through our Lord Jesus Christ, who died, was buried, and was raised again for us.
To him be glory for ever and ever.

Or:

Now we commend our *sister/brother* into God's care and commit —— to be *cremated/buried*, trusting in God's love and compassion.

After a brief silence, there may follow whatever prayers and reflections seem appropriate.

Silence

Prayers and Reflections

You, Christ, are the king of glory,
the eternal Son of the Father.
When you took our flesh to set us free
you humbly chose the Virgin's womb.
You overcame the sting of death
and opened the kingdom of heaven to all believers.

You are seated at God's right hand in glory.
We believe that you will come to be our judge.
   Come then, Lord, and help your people,
   bought with the price of your own blood,
   and bring us with your saints
   to glory everlasting.

God be in my head, and in my understanding;
God be in mine eyes, and in my looking;
God be in my mouth, and in my speaking;
God be in my heart, and in my thinking;
God be at mine end, and at my departing.

Eternal God and Father,
you create us by your power
and redeem us by your love;
guide and strengthen us by your Spirit,
that we may give ourselves in love and service
to one another and to you;
through Jesus Christ our Lord.

Ascription of Glory and/or Blessing

To him who is able to keep you from falling, and to
bring you faultless and joyful before his glorious
presence, to the only God, our Saviour, through Jesus
Christ our Lord, be glory, majesty, might, and
authority, from all ages past, and now, and for ever
and ever! Amen.   *Jude 24–25*

May the peace of God, which is beyond our utmost
understanding and of far more worth than human
reasoning, keep guard over our hearts and thoughts; in
Christ Jesus our Lord.   *Based on Philippians 4: 7*

May the God of hope fill you with all joy and peace in believing, so that by the power of the Holy Spirit you may abound in hope.   *Romans 15: 13*

For the Burial or Scattering of Ashes

This brief service, usually in the open air, has no fixed pattern. It may include a reading of scripture, words of committal or commendation and a prayer.

Sentences

We brought nothing into this world, and we can take nothing out.
The Lord gives and the Lord takes away;
blessed be the name of the Lord.

                    1 Timothy 6: 7; Job 1: 21

The Lord is faithful to all his promises
and loving towards all he has made.
The Lord upholds all those who fall
and lifts up all who are bowed down.   *Psalm 145: 13–14*

All you have made will praise you, O Lord;
your saints will extol you.
They will tell of the glory of your kingdom
and speak of your might,
so that all may know of your mighty acts
and the glorious splendour of your kingdom.
The Lord is near to all who call on him,
to all who call on him in truth.

My mouth will speak in praise of the Lord.
Let every creature praise his holy name
for ever and ever.   *Psalm 145: 10–12, 18, 21*

Interment

We have entrusted our *sister/brother* —— to God's
merciful care. *We now commit his/her* ashes to the
ground, trusting in God the creator of all things, and in
his redeeming purpose.

> *Or:*

Scattering of Ashes

We have entrusted our *sister/brother* —— to God's
merciful care. *We now commit his/her* ashes to the
earth, trusting in God whose spirit is at work
fashioning a new creation.

Prayer

We remember —— with gratitude and affection, and
give thanks for *him/her*. We say again that this is not
the end, for our God is the God who raised Jesus from
the dead and will bring us all to life.
Lord, we remember your love toward us and all people,
especially your love for your *daughter/son* ——.
We give you thanks that your love never comes to an
end, that whether we live or die we belong to you.
We give you thanks for all that —— still means to us,
and we pray for ourselves, that we may continue to
grow in love until we reach the full stature of Christ, in
whom all things are one; we ask it in his name.

Additional material for situations of particular pastoral need

Pastoral notes, scripture sentences and prayers are offered here for use with other material. The situations addressed are the funerals of:

> a still-born or newly born child;
>
> a child;
>
> the victim of sudden or violent death;
>
> a person who has committed suicide.

In such distressing circumstances, such as the death of a child or a sudden death, the role of the minister is not to stand in place of God, finding answers for the worshippers. Instead, he or she is called to point them to the presence of God who stands alongside them in their grief. When a death seems senseless, such feelings should be expressed, while at the same time asking for God's help and an assurance of his love and grace.

Memorial Service for a Public Tragedy

Material from various sections may prove helpful in preparing for a public memorial service after a major disaster. On such an occasion, there is need for a public expression of grief which allows those affected to mark the occasion collectively and to feel that what they have gone through has not gone unnoticed.

A memorial service is not a funeral. Funerals are personal and relate more immediately to the release of the body. A memorial service is part of the reflective and healing process. Survivors need time to recover physically, and the service may be three, six, or even twelve months after the event.

Preparation should involve consultation with the bereaved and representatives of the community may be invited to take part. The names of those who have died should be mentioned at some point or written in the order of service. Onlookers and those who helped in a rescue should not be overlooked as they too have been affected and need to feel a part of what is being expressed. All this underlines that such a service will be specially planned and involve wide consultation. However, there may well be material in this section which can be used or adapted.

Prayer of Confession *for use when a sense of guilt or inadequacy is felt by the mourners*

Father God, our love is imperfect and our friendship is unreliable; forgive us for the failings of our relationships with ——
For leaving things unsaid, forgive us.
For speaking too soon, forgive us.
For opportunities missed, forgive us.
For things better left undone, forgive us.
For love we lacked, and love we hid, forgive us.
Father God,
By your love which does not fail and now holds —— secure,
cover our faults, renew, and remake us, and guide us in all the future until we come, with ——, into the joy and unity of your presence; through Jesus Christ our Lord.

For a Still-Born or Newly Born Child

In the funeral for a baby it is important to recognize and express the belief that the baby was a person. Even if he or she never lived outside the womb, he or she was a loved child who has died. The use of the child's name will therefore be important. The care and love given to the child should be affirmed, especially if there are lingering feelings of guilt on the part of the parents about the quality of care they gave.

Scripture Sentences

The Lord's true love is surely not spent, nor has his compassion failed; they are new every morning, so great is his constancy.   *Lamentations 3: 22–23*

Cast your burden on the Lord, and he will sustain you.
                                                                        Psalm 55: 22

God has said, 'I will never leave you: I will never abandon you.'   *Hebrews 13: 5*

The Lamb who is at the throne will be their shepherd and will lead them to springs of living water; and God will wipe away all tears from their eyes.
                                                                    Revelation 7: 17

Scripture Readings *might include part of Psalm 139; Mark 10: 13–16; John 1: 1–5; Ephesians 3: 14–19*

Prayers

Living God, loving Father, be with us to give us the courage and hope of your promises. You have invited us to unload our burdens on to you because you will support us: fulfil that promise now.

Go with us on our way as we pay these last offices of love, and assure us again that you are our home, and that underneath us are the everlasting arms.

So we shall leave the one we love in your keeping,
believing that you are bringing *him/her* and us to
undying life with Jesus Christ our Lord.

Father in heaven, healer of broken hearts,
we ask you to look in pity and compassion upon your
servants whose joy has been turned into mourning.
Comfort them and grant that they may be drawn closer
together by their common sorrow. Dwell with them
and be their refuge until the day breaks and the
shadows flee away; through Jesus Christ our Lord.

Heavenly Father, you have given us life and in Jesus
you promise us new life which nothing can destroy.
We entrust —— into your loving care: greet *him/her*
with your love and surround *him/her* with your healing
power, that *he/she* may live in your presence as a whole
child of God, for your glory and delight; through Jesus
Christ our Lord.

Almighty God, you make nothing in vain, and love all
that you have made.
Comfort these parents in their sorrow, and console
them by the knowledge of your unfailing love;
through Jesus Christ our Lord.

On the Death of a Child

*If other children are present at this service, their grief
should be recognized and the language used should
enable them to share as much as possible. The
following prayers try to take account of this pastoral
need.*

Sentences

The Sovereign Lord is coming to rule with power.
He will take care of his flock like a shepherd; he will
gather the lambs together and carry them in his arms.

Isaiah 40: 10–11

Jesus said, 'Never despise one of these little ones. It is
not your heavenly Father's will that one of these little
ones should be lost.' *Matthew 18: 10, 14*

Scripture Readings *might include Matthew 18: 1–5; 18:
10–14; Mark 10: 13–16; 2 Corinthians 1: 1–3.*

Prayers

Father God, we are glad that —— no longer has to
know pain or fear, but we are sad for ourselves that
he/she is no longer with us to share things together and
to have fun with us.
Father God, we are very unhappy: we cannot
understand what has happened to ——.
Please help us to know that however hard it is for us,
he/she is being looked after by you and that you love
him/her still more than we do.
We believe that you are looking after *him/her*; please
look after us as well; through Jesus Christ our Lord.

Father God, we thank you for ——.
We thank you for all the enjoyment *he/she* found in . . .
(here favourite activities or games may be mentioned).
Thank you for all the pleasure and love that ——
brought to us and the way in which caring for *him/her*
helped us to grow. We thank you for the things *he/she*

taught us and the things which *he/she* said and did
which will stay with us for ever.

Thank you for giving —— to us. Help us to learn to
live without *him/her*, yet still remembering *him/her*
with love and gratitude; through Jesus Christ our Lord.

In the awfulness of life cut short, let us turn to God,
the Father of our Lord Jesus Christ and our Father.
We try so hard to be strong before others, but, in the
presence of God who understands all things, let us
admit our weakness and our need of help.

   Silence

Father God, we pray for ourselves and especially for
those who suffer most at ——'s death. Even if we can
grasp nothing else at this time, help us to know that
you are near and that you will lead us onward; through
Jesus Christ our Lord.

For a Sudden or Violent Death

*Where death is very sudden, the prevailing emotion of
the mourners may well be one of shock and disbelief.
The funeral may be an important opportunity for
friends and family to be set free from that initial
disbelief and to begin to grieve.*

*If a person is the victim of a criminal act or of
carelessness on the part of others, the feelings of the
family towards those who may be responsible should
be dealt with sensitively. Care must be taken with the
manner in which the Christian call to forgive is
expressed.*

Sentences

God is our refuge and strength; a very present help in trouble. Therefore we will not fear, though the earth be moved and though the mountains are shaken in the midst of the sea; though the waters rage and foam and though the mountains quake at the rising of the sea.

Psalm 46: 1–3

Christ died for us while we were yet sinners, and that is God's proof of his love towards us. *Romans 5: 8*

Scripture Readings *may include Psalm 22: 19–27 or Romans 8: 18, 28, 35, 37–39.*

Prayers

Our Father, we believe your promises of victory, but we did not want to hear them for —— just yet. There is so much unfinished business and we find it hard to accept that it will not now be completed as we would have wished.

Help us in this act of worship to let go of all such burdens and allow you to come near to us in the aching void of loss; through Jesus Christ our Lord.

Lord, we thank you for ——. Thank you for *him/her* as a person, for all *his/her* qualities and for all *he/she* meant to us.

We entrust *him/her* into your hands, knowing that you alone are the one to satisfy the longings of *his/her* heart.

Lord, you are the one who brings good out of evil, so

now we pray that you will bring something good out of
——'s tragic death.

We pray for all those touched by ——'s life and death.
Help us to hear what you are saying to us. Turn us
away from all that we know to be wrong. Help us to
show love and understanding to those around us.

Forgive us for any ways in which we may have hurt
——.

Help us to know that you are always ready to forgive
us and offer us a new beginning when we turn to you.
Keep us in your grace, guide and protect us, until with
—— and with all your children we find ourselves truly
at home in your great love; through Jesus Christ our
Lord.

God of compassion, you know us better than we know
ourselves. You understand what we are feeling and are
with us in our grief. Bind the wounds of our sorrow
and surround us with your love; through Jesus Christ
our Lord.

For the victim of violence

Prayers

Eternal God, the savagery that has taken —— has
wounded us as well. We are reeling under the blow,
unable to think clearly and aware of the cruel ways life
can end. In all the anger and perplexity of this time,
help us to cling to you as the calm at the centre of the
storm; through Jesus Christ our Lord.

Almighty God, we know that we should forgive those
who have so defied your laws about the sanctity of

human life, but the pain and the anger seem too great. For now, we ask you to do for us what we cannot do for ourselves: forgive those who have committed this crime and heal that which is flawed in them.

We also pray that you will help us to forgive, that we may be set free from bitterness and know your peace; through Jesus Christ our Lord.

After a Suicide

In these circumstances it is pastorally dangerous to ask too many questions in the service or seem to be making judgements about what led to the ending of the person's life or its consequences.

Mourners may be carrying a heavy burden of guilt and opportunity for confession may be important with a stress on God's forgiveness.

It is important that the manner of a person's death should not overshadow all that has been good in their life. Their qualities and gifts deserve as much affirmation as those of any other person.

Sentences

A voice cries: 'In the wilderness prepare the way of the Lord; the uneven ground shall become level, and the rough places plain'. *Isaiah 40: 3, 4*

Lord, you have examined me and you know me. You know me at rest and in action; you discern my thoughts from afar. You trace my journeying and my resting-places, and are familiar with all the paths I take.

Examine me, O God, and know my thoughts; test me and understand my misgivings. *Psalm 139: 1–3, 23*

I will not leave you bereft; I am coming back to you.
Peace is my parting gift to you, my own peace, such as
the world cannot give. Set your troubled hearts at rest,
and banish your fears.   *John 14: 18, 27*

Scripture Readings *may include Psalms 22: 1–4; 23: 1–4;*
Wisdom 3: 1–3

Prayers

Lord, we do not understand what has happened. There
seems to be no sense in the ending of this life and we
are puzzled and distressed.

In the crucifixion of Jesus you have shown us that your
love is alongside us even when we feel abandoned. As
we remember —— and think of the despair which must
have engulfed *him/her* at the end, help us to realize that
there is nothing more powerful than your love.

We thank you for the good things in ——'s life and ask
forgiveness for those times when we let *him/her* down.
Forgive our sins and heal our guilt, we pray.

Redeemer God, take what has happened and somehow
weave it into your loving purpose, so that —— may not
have lived or died in vain. This we ask in the name of
Jesus our Saviour.

>   *Or:*

Lord Jesus Christ, you spoke of your Father's love for
all people; help us to know that your love will never be
withdrawn from —— or from us.

Lord Jesus Christ, you wrestled with questions of life
and death in Gethsemane; help us to know that you
understand and are present where there is anguish of
mind.

Lord Jesus Christ, you gave hope beyond death to a dying man on a cross; help us to know that you did not withdraw hope from ——.

Lord Jesus Christ, we pray for ourselves and for all who are bereft at this time, knowing that you have experienced all the depths of life and believing that you still call us to experience its everlasting heights.

MINISTRY

The fundamental ministry in the Christian Church is exercised by God in Christ towards his children. It is a ministry in which all Christians are called to share through the work of the Holy Spirit. Baptists have always expressed this conviction by their emphasis on the priesthood of all believers, the corporate ministry of the whole Church. They also believe that God calls some men and women to particular types of ministry within the Body of Christ.

In this section the focus is on those services that underline particular callings to ministry.

- Firstly, there is material for commissioning to ministries recognized within the context of the local church.

- Secondly, there is material for the ordination and induction of those who have been called to recognized pastoral ministry within the Baptist Union of Great Britain.

- Thirdly, a pattern is offered for an act of commissioning for those whose ministry will be other than local, e.g. Union, College, or Association appointments.

- Fourthly, a pattern of service is offered for those about to embark on ministry with the Baptist Missionary Society or with a similar body.

Commissioning within the Local Church

Commissioning of local church workers within the context of worship (preferably at the Lord's Supper) is appropriate when the church meeting has previously called a person to a position of leadership and responsibility.

The minister or leader introduces each worker by name, indicates the office or work to which he or she has been called, and expresses the welcome and prayerful support of the church. Then follow scripture readings and prayer, which may be accompanied by the laying on of hands.

A full pattern is offered here for the commissioning of elders and deacons. This may be adapted for other offices and the suggested scripture readings and extra prayers incorporated.

LEADER In the name of the Lord Jesus Christ we are now to receive and welcome these friends whom the Church Meeting has called to serve as *deacons/elders.*

(Here the minister reads the names of the deacons or elders, making reference to any particular sphere of service, such as Secretary, Treasurer, etc.)

As servants of Christ in this church, they are called to share with the minister in the tasks of pastoral leadership and administration. Trust them and pray for them, and at all times help them in the work of the Lord.

One or more of the following scripture passages is

*read: Mark 10: 43–51; Acts 6: 1–6; Romans
12: 1–4, 6, 7, 11; Ephesians 4: 1–3; 4: 11–13;
1 Peter 4: 10–11.*

LEADER My *brother(s)/sister(s)*, do you believe in one
God, Father, Son, and Holy Spirit, and do you
confess Jesus Christ as your Saviour and Lord?

DEACON(S)/ELDERS(S) *I/we* do so believe and confess.

LEADER Do you believe that God has called you
through his church to this office, and do you
promise, in dependence upon his grace, to exercise
this ministry faithfully?

DEACONS/ELDERS *I/We* do.

*The Leader then prays extempore or as follows.
The laying on of hands may take place here.*

Our Father and our God, we thank you for these
brothers/sisters whom you have called to service. Thank
you for their individual gifts and qualities and for their
strength as a team. As we set them apart for this
ministry, we ask for your blessing on them. Guide and
equip them by your Spirit that your church may grow
in wisdom, love, and unity, and that your name may be
glorified; through Jesus Christ our Lord.

*The Leader shall then (on behalf of the church)
give the right hand of fellowship to the
deacons/elders, saying:*

In the name of Jesus Christ and on behalf of his church
in this place, welcome to this office of *elder/deacon*.
May God bless you as you carry out all your duties.

CONGREGATION   May the Lord bless you and keep
you;

The Lord make his face to shine upon
you and be gracious to you;
The Lord turn his face towards you
and give you peace.

Scripture Passages for Other Offices

Children's leaders: *Deuteronomy 6: 4–9; 6: 20,
21, 23; Matthew 19: 14; Mark 9: 37; 1 Timothy
4: 16.*

Youth workers: *Matthew 20: 26–29; 23: 11–12;
Galatians 6: 9; 2 Timothy 2: 1–7.*

Preachers: *Isaiah 52: 7; 1 Corinthians 1: 17;
2: 1–2; 2 Corinthians 4: 5–6; 2 Timothy 2: 15;
4: 1, 2, 5.*

Music leaders: *Psalms 96: 1–2; 100: 1; 150: 1–2,
6; Ephesians 5: 18b–19.*

Housegroup leaders: *Romans 12: 1, 6, 11, 12;
Colossians 3: 17; 1 Peter 4: 10–11b; Hebrews
13: 20–21.*

Ordination and Induction

In ordination a person's call from God to the pastoral
ministry of Word and Sacrament is given public recognition as he or she is set apart to serve and to lead. The
ordination service acts as a focal point after years of
prayerful preparation. It is desirable that those who have
shared in this process take part in the service, particularly
in the laying on of hands. Care should be taken to reflect
in the service that ordained ministry is part of the corporate ministry of the church, and is to be exercised beyond

the local church. Ordination is to the Christian ministry generally, whereas induction is a service of recognition and commissioning for ministry within the local church.

Induction is a service not only for the newly appointed minister, but also for the church with whom he or she will share in ministry. A Baptist minister can be appointed only by the Church Meeting, and traditionally this has been expressed by an account of the call to the pastorate, given by the church secretary (or other church representative) and by the new minister. Links which the local church has with other Baptists and other Christians or community groups should find expression in the right hand of fellowship proffered within the act of worship or by greetings being given at a gathering after the service.

There has always been a variety of Baptist practice in ordination and induction. At the beginning of a person's ministry ordination and induction may take place in one service at the calling church. Alternatively an ordination may be held separately at the church which has sent the person to prepare for ministry (although ordination only takes place after a specific call to service has been both issued and accepted).

Leadership in such services also varies. In the ordination service the importance of the preparation process for ministry is generally reflected by the involvement of a College Principal or Tutor, or other person concerned with ministerial training. The importance of the wider Baptist family is expressed by the participation of a General Superintendent, or other Union or Association representative in an induction service. Some believe that the General Superintendent should preside over the ordination. There will usually be other participants in the service and consideration should be given to their appropriate roles. No effort has been made to prescribe those roles here: instead, the term 'leader' has been used in the ordination material.

Material is offered for a service of ordination, a service of induction, and a service in which both acts take place. The patterns below suggest some ways in which the acts of ordination and induction may be incorporated into an act of worship. The detailed material which follows is not tied to a particular format. Two sets of promises are offered for ordination services and two sets for induction services, and these are interchangeable.

A Service of Ordination

Call to Worship

Hymn

Prayers of Approach

Old Testament Reading

Hymn

New Testament Reading

Sermon

Hymn

FIRST PATTERN OF ORDINATION

> **Introductory statement**
> **Statements concerning the call and its testing**
> **Questions to the ordinand**
> **Presentation of ordination bible**
> **Laying on of hands and ordination prayer**

Declaration of ordination

Hymn

Prayers of Intercession

Offering

Hymn[1]

Blessing[2]

A Service of Induction

Call to worship

Hymn

Prayers of Adoration and Confession

Old Testament reading

New Testament reading

Hymn/Song

FIRST PATTERN OF INDUCTION

 Presentation of minister

 Induction promises

 Induction prayer

 Declaration of induction

---

[1] The service may proceed with the Lord's Supper led by the newly ordained minister.

[2] Normally said by the newly ordained minister.

Prayer of blessing

Expressions of welcome

Hymn

Sermon

Prayers for ourselves and others

Hymn

Blessing

A Service of Ordination and Induction

Call to worship

Time of praise

Scripture readings

Prayers for God's blessing on the service

SECOND PATTERN OF ORDINATION

Statement concerning service of ordination and induction

Questions to the ordinand

Presentation of the ordinand

Laying on of hands[3] **and prayer**

---

[3] The belief of the Christian Church concerning the laying on of hands is that it reflects the practice of the early Church. In the New Testament the laying on of hands was a focus of prayer and of the action of the Holy Spirit. It marked both a setting apart and a sending out.

Some feel that this practice should only take place at ordination.

Presentation of ordination bible

Hymn/Song

SECOND PATTERN OF INDUCTION

    Statement by church secretary

    Statement by minister

    Questions to minister and church members

    Induction prayer

    Declaration of ordination and induction

    Giving of right hand of fellowship

Prayers for the minister, church, and local community

Hymn

Sermon

Hymn

Blessing

Scripture passages for Ordination and Induction Services

Numbers 11: 16, 17, 24–30; Isaiah 6: 1–8; 61: 1–11; Jeremiah 1: 4–10; Matthew 4: 12–25; 9: 35–10: 16;

Others feel that it is appropriate at a point of commissioning for new service: they may therefore wish to include the laying on of hands at induction services throughout their ministry.

The laying on of hands is a community event, its participants acting on behalf of others. Therefore it is important that the wider as well as the local Christian Church should be represented, and that, in order to reflect the priesthood of all believers, participants should not only be those who have been ordained.

28: 16–20; Luke 5: 1–11; 10: 1–22; 12: 35–48; John 10: 1–18; 21: 15–19; Romans 10: 6–17; 12: 1–21; 1 Corinthians 12: 1–11; 2 Corinthians 4: 1–18; 5: 11–21; 6: 1–10; Ephesians 3: 7–12; 4: 1–16; 1 Timothy 6: 11–16; 2 Timothy 1: 3–14; 2: 1–13; 4: 1–8; 1 Peter 5: 1–11.

First Pattern of Ordination

Introductory Statement

LEADER We meet today in the name of almighty God to set —— apart for the pastoral ministry of Word and Sacrament, believing that God has so called *him/her.*

It is right that we who are gathered in this congregation, as representative members of the Church of Christ, should hear —— give an account of *his/her* call.

Then we should hear from those who have sought, under the guidance of the Holy Spirit, to test that call, who have recognized it to be from God, and who now commend ——'s suitability for this ministry.

Statements concerning the call and its testing may follow from the ordinand, the Church Secretary of his or her home church, an officer from the commending Association, a representative of his or her College, or other person involved in his or her preparation for ministry, and the church secretary of his or her calling church.

Or the following words may be used:

LEADER ——, in the presence of God and before his people, you come today to be ordained to the ministry to which God has called you. Do you believe that God has given you this calling?

ORDINAND I do.

(This statement should be expanded to include personal details of how God's call was perceived and answered)

LEADER TO REPRESENTATIVE OF THE HOME CHURCH ——, you represent the local church of which —— was a member when *he/she* responded to the call to the ministry. Are you able to confirm that the members of the church recognized God at work in this?

HOME CHURCH REPRESENTATIVE I am. —— was received into membership of —— Baptist Church, *upon his/her baptism/following his/her baptism/by transfer of membership having been baptized in* —— *Church*. As *he/she* played *his/her* part in the life and ministry of our church, the members recognized *his/her* calling and gladly commended *him/her* for preparation for ordination.

LEADER TO REPRESENTATIVE OF COMMENDING ASSOCIATION ——, you represent —— Baptist Association which was charged with testing ——'s call to the Baptist ministry. As a fellowship of churches do you believe that God has set *him/her* apart to serve the body of Christ?

ASSOCIATION REPRESENTATIVE We do. Our ministerial recognition committee heard from those who know ——'s character and conduct, and talked with —— about *his/her* calling, and how *he/she* should respond. We were glad to commend *him/her* for further training and are glad today to give witness to *his/her* calling from God.

LEADER TO COLLEGE REPRESENTATIVE[4] —— has prepared for the ministry at —— College. —— as ——, do you confirm that the College now recommends *him/her* as a minister in the Church of Christ?

COLLEGE/TRAINING REPRESENTATIVE I do. —— has studied the Scriptures so that *he/she* might be well grounded in the Word of God. *He/she* has received training in pastoral care and leadership, all the while being encouraged to grow in Christian character. From study of the thought and practice of the wider Church of God, and from *his/her* further experience of its life, *he/she* has learnt of the work of the Spirit of God throughout the ages and among different peoples, so that *he/she* is better able to serve the church in whatever locality God may require. We believe that —— has been called by God to this ministry and we commend *him/her* to the churches.

LEADER TO REPRESENTATIVE OF CALLING CHURCH[5] The call to be a minister in the Church of Christ must be confirmed through an invitation to serve in the

[4] These paragraphs will be adapted appropriately for those who took Baptist Union approved routes to ordination other than through Baptist Colleges.

[5] These paragraphs will be adapted if the community to which the candidate is called, and which is recognized by the Baptist Union as a proper sphere for ordained ministry, is other than a local congregation.

fellowship and mission of a particular Christian community. —— has been invited to the pastorate of —— Church. ——, as *secretary/representative* of that church, do you confirm that its members believe this to be in the purpose of God?

CALLING CHURCH REPRESENTATIVE I do. —— met with us and we spent time together exploring our vision for the future. *He/she* led us in worship and shared with us *his/her* own hopes for future ministry. In Church Meeting we agreed it to be the will of God that we should invite *him/her* to minister among us.

Questions to the Ordinand

LEADER My *brother/sister*, do you believe in one God, Father, Son, and Holy Spirit, and do you confess Jesus Christ as your Saviour and Lord?

ORDINAND I do so believe and confess.

LEADER Jesus told his followers, 'Go to all peoples everywhere and make them my disciples'. In your ministry will you seek to ensure that the gospel of Jesus Christ is proclaimed in such a way that many may hear and understand his good news for them?

ORDINAND I will.

LEADER Jesus said to Peter, 'feed my sheep'. In your ministry will you play your part in the nourishment and nurture of the flock of Christ that the members may be able to grow to maturity and use the gifts Christ has entrusted to them?

ORDINAND I will.

LEADER Jesus commanded his disciples, 'love one another as I have loved you'. In your ministry will you do your best to ensure that the welcome and help of the church will be available for all who seek it, whatever their need or circumstance?

ORDINAND I will.

LEADER Jesus challenged his disciples to leave self behind, to take up their cross, and to follow after him. Are you determined to walk this path even though you do not know where it leads?

ORDINAND I am.

Presentation of Ordination Bible *(normally by College representative)*

Receive this copy of the Scriptures. Study them so that you may grow in Christ and may help the Church to proclaim the whole truth of God for the world.

Laying on of Hands and Ordination Prayer *(candidate kneels, holding bible)*

Prayer is offered extempore or as follows:

Almighty Father, we praise and glorify you because you sent your only Son Jesus Christ to be the servant of all, and because Jesus who has died is risen and reigning and calls women and men to follow him today.

Now we ask you to anoint this your servant —— with your Holy Spirit as we ordain *him/her* in your name to share in the ministry of Christ. Send upon *him/her* the Spirit of wisdom to proclaim the good news of forgiveness of sins through Jesus; send upon *him/her* the Spirit of love to bring healing to those who are broken; send upon *him/her* the Spirit of power to challenge all who oppress the weak. Keep *him/her* faithful in times of trial and testing, always abounding in hope and filled with the grace of Jesus Christ our Lord, to whom be glory for ever and ever.

Declaration of Ordination

LEADER In the name of God the Father, the Son, and the Holy Spirit, we declare you to be a minister in the Church of Jesus Christ. We affirm that you are appointed to serve in the churches of the Baptist Union of Great Britain.

CONGREGATION ——, may the Lord bless you and keep you; The Lord make his face to shine upon you and be gracious to you;
The Lord turn his face towards you and give you peace.

First Pattern of Induction

Presentation of Minister

The congregation being seated, the secretary and treasurer (representing the church fellowship) will present the minister-elect to the General Superintendent, and the church secretary will say:

We present to you, on behalf of the members of —— Church, ——.
Believing that we are guided by the Spirit of God, we have called *him/her* to be our pastor. We

therefore ask you to induct *him/her* to the
pastorate of this church.

Induction Promises

GENERAL SUPERINTENDENT My *sister/brother*, seeing
that we are about to appoint you to this charge,
and that you have been called by God to this
ministry, I ask you in his name, do you believe in
one God, Father, Son, and Holy Spirit, and do
you confess Jesus Christ as your Saviour and
Lord?

MINISTER-ELECT I do.

GENERAL SUPERINTENDENT Do you believe in your
heart that you have been called by God to the
pastoral oversight of this church and
congregation?

MINISTER-ELECT I do.

GENERAL SUPERINTENDENT As you serve among this
church family will you be committed to giving to
its members and to receiving from them? Will you
obey the call to lead this fellowship whilst
continuing to follow our Lord Jesus Christ who is
the Head of the Church?

MINISTER-ELECT I will, relying on God's help.

*(For use with a leadership team, such as
deacons/elders/other church workers)*

GENERAL SUPERINTENDENT Do you believe in your
hearts you have been truly called by God to work
with each other and with this church and
congregation?

TEAM MEMBERS We do.

GENERAL SUPERINTENDENT Do you pledge yourselves to work together humbly and cheerfully, that by the grace of God you may each fully use the gifts he has given to you and thus reflect his glory?

TEAM MEMBERS With God's help, we will.

(Optional question for minister's spouse)

SUPERINTENDENT ——, you have heard the commitment that —— has made to this church.
Do you promise to encourage and support *him/her* as *he/she* seeks to exercise *his/her* ministry in this church and community?

SPOUSE Relying on God's help, I will.

(Members of the church stand)

GENERAL SUPERINTENDENT My sisters and brothers, together you are making an important act of commitment believing that you have been called by God to work with this minister. In God's name I ask you, do you believe in one God, Father, Son, and Holy Spirit, and do you confess Jesus Christ as your Saviour and Lord?

CHURCH MEMBERS We do.

GENERAL SUPERINTENDENT Do you, the members of this church, acknowledge and receive —— as your minister?

CHURCH MEMBERS We do.

GENERAL SUPERINTENDENT Will you honour and support *him/her*, working together humbly and cheerfully as the people of God?

CHURCH MEMBERS We will.

(Whole congregation stands)

GENERAL SUPERINTENDENT As representatives of the
        wider Church, do you support this new chapter in
        the life of church and minister?

CONGREGATION We do.

GENERAL SUPERINTENDENT Will you continue to offer
        your love and prayer and encouragement to this
        fellowship in the months and years ahead?

CONGREGATION We will.

> *(Congregation remains standing)*
>
> *Induction prayer (extempore or as follows) will
> then be offered by the General Superintendent.*

O God our Father, we give you thanks that on this day
of new beginnings we can look forward to new
opportunities sent by you. We pray particularly for ——
as *he/she* is inducted to the pastorate of this church and
congregation, and commits *himself/herself* to leadership
and partnership with your people here.

Grant to *him/her* the blessing and gifts of your Holy
Spirit, so that *he/she* may worthily and faithfully do the
work to which you have called *him/her*.

In preaching and teaching give to *him/her* wisdom and
understanding. In pastoral care and leadership may
he/she be filled with the compassion and vision of
Christ. In the tasks of mission and all the varied
concerns of your kingdom enable *him/her* to discern
and do your holy will.

Keep alive *his/her* sense of your call and of your
strengthening presence and peace.

For *him/her* and for all your church here we ask that
mutual trust and love will help them to maintain the

unity of the Spirit in the bond of peace, so that the ministry which they share may be fruitful and full of blessing to many people; through Jesus Christ our Lord.

Declaration of Induction

GENERAL SUPERINTENDENT In the name of our Lord Jesus Christ, in the name of this church, and in the name of the Baptist Union of Great Britain, I now declare that —— has been inducted to the pastorate of this church and congregation, to work with the members in the ministry to which Christ has called them all. As a token of this I now give the right hand of fellowship.

Church members and minister remain standing for the blessing, which may be said by the rest of the congregation.

Prayer of Blessing *(for church and minister)*

May the Lord bless you and keep you;
the Lord make his face to shine upon you and be gracious to you;
the Lord turn his face towards you and give you peace.

Church Secretary then leads an expression of welcome to the minister and his or her household on the part of the church: Gifts may be presented as a token of welcome—this could be an opportunity to involve the children of the church.

CHURCH SECRETARY —— *(names all minister's household)*
We are glad to be your new church family and

together we want to show our friendship and to say:

CHURCH AND CONGREGATION In the name of Christ, welcome.

Representatives of other groups may now express their welcome with the right hand of fellowship. Alternatively, this could take place at a gathering held after the service.

If desired, prayers for the minister, church, and local community may be offered here, possibly led by different people.

Blessing

May the God of hope fill you all with joy and peace in believing, that you may abound in hope, through the power of the Holy Spirit.　　　　　*Romans 15: 13*

A Service of Ordination and Induction

See pages 174–5 for a suggested pattern of worship. What follows here is an introductory statement for the whole service, and material for the second pattern of ordination and the second pattern of induction.

Statement Concerning the Service

LEADER We meet today in the name of almighty God at the request of this church and as representatives of the fellowship of churches of the Baptist Union of Great Britain that, in accordance with the practice of the Christian Church from its earliest days, we may ordain —— to the work of Christian ministry and induct *him/her* as pastor of this church and congregation.

He/she is being ordained to preach and teach the Word of God, to lead the church in worship and mission, to administer the Sacraments of Baptism and the Lord's Supper, and to be a faithful pastor of the people of God.

Ordination rests upon the call of God acknowledged and confirmed by the Church. —— shall first declare that *he/she* believes *he/she* is called by God to this ministry and that *he/she* will be faithful and conscientious in *his/her* work. The local church shall then declare that, being gathered together under the guidance of the Holy Spirit, the members have called *him/her* to be their minister and that they welcome *him/her* in the name of the Lord.

Second Pattern of Ordination

Questions to the Ordinand

LEADER Do you believe in one God, Father, Son, and Holy Spirit, and do you confess Jesus Christ as your Saviour and Lord?

ORDINAND I do.

LEADER Do you believe that you are called by God to this ministry?

ORDINAND I believe that God has called me.

LEADER Do you accept the Scriptures as revealing the truth concerning the salvation offered to us through our Lord Jesus Christ?

ORDINAND I do.

Optional question for use where it is felt to be appropriate.

LEADER *As members of the Baptist Union of Great Britain, we make this Declaration of Principle. (The Declaration of Principle is read aloud — see page 204).*
Are you in whole-hearted agreement with this statement?

ORDINAND *I am.*

Presentation of the Ordinand

LEADER Those whose duty it is to enquire about —— and examine *him/her* have recognized *his/her* commitment to the pilgrimage of Christian faith, and believe *him/her* to be duly called to serve God in this ministry. It is therefore your will that *he/she* should be ordained?

CONGREGATION It is.

LEADER Will you uphold *him/her* in this ministry?

CONGREGATION We will.

Laying on of Hands

LEADER Following the practice of the early church we set —— apart by the laying on of hands. Representatives of the wider Church, and also of the sending and calling churches, will share in this act, for we are ordaining —— to Christian ministry in the wider fellowship of churches of our Baptist faith and order.

Ordination Prayer *said during the laying on of hands, extempore or as follows:*

LEADER Our Father God, we now set apart your servant —— in the name of Jesus for the work of ministry. We ask that *he/she* may know the presence and power of your Spirit. Guide and direct *him/her* as *he/she* seeks to lead your people. Make *him/her* a wise and able teacher, fill *him/her* with your love that *he/she* may be a good pastor, and enable *him/her* to lead in mission and ministry that your name may be glorified. Keep *him/her* faithful in times of testing, humble in times of success, and joyful in your service; through Jesus Christ our Lord.

Presentation of Ordination Bible

This is normally done by a College representative, with an appropriate word of encouragement and/or verse of scripture.

*Here a hymn or song may be sung, after which
the General Superintendent shall lead the act of
induction.*

Second Pattern of Induction

GENERAL SUPERINTENDENT We come now to the act of
   induction to the pastorate of this church. We shall
   hear first how the church felt led to call —— to be
   their minister, and then from —— why *he/she*
   responded to the call.

Statement by Church Secretary *detailing how the church
came to issue the call to the minister.*

Statement by Minister *detailing how he or she recognized the
call and responded to it.*

Questions to Minister and Church Members

SUPERINTENDENT TO THE MINISTER My *sister/brother*,
   are you convinced that you have been called by
   God to serve him through the pastoral oversight
   of his people here?

MINISTER I am.

SUPERINTENDENT Do you promise to carry out this
   ministry with enthusiasm and dedication, to set
   God's Word before his people, to lead in the
   conduct of worship, to work in partnership with
   the *elders/deacons* and members of the fellowship,
   and to encourage and enable them all to carry out
   Christ's mission in the local community and the
   world?

MINISTER Relying on God's help I make this solemn promise.

SUPERINTENDENT Will you be conscientious in prayer, in reading the scriptures, and in all studies that will deepen your faith and help you to uphold the truth of the Gospel?

MINISTER Relying on God's help I will.

SUPERINTENDENT TO THE CHURCH MEMBERS Brothers and sisters in Christ, do you acknowledge and receive —— as your minister?

CHURCH MEMBERS We do.

SUPERINTENDENT Will you encourage and support *him/her* in *his/her* ministry, and will you play your part alongside *him/her* in forwarding the work of the Kingdom of God?

CHURCH MEMBERS Gladly we will.

The Superintendent then asks the congregation to stand.

Induction Prayer *extempore or as follows:*

Our Father God, we give you thanks for the guidance of your Holy Spirit that has brought this church and this minister together today. Bless them in their life together. May they be humble as they seek your will and bold as they proclaim your message of salvation. We ask that the promises that they have made today will direct their conduct in the future, and that their partnership in the work of your Church and kingdom will bring blessing to many people and praise to your name.

To you be the glory, in the church, and in Christ Jesus, from generation to generation for evermore.

Declaration of Induction and Ordination

In the name of our Lord Jesus Christ, in the name of this church, and in the name of the churches of our Baptist faith and order, we declare you to be ordained to the Christian ministry and inducted as pastor of this church.

May the Lord bless your going out and coming in now and for evermore.

The Right Hand of Fellowship

This may now be given by the General Superintendent, and then by various representatives if desired.

Ministry Beyond the Local Church

When a person is called to ministry beyond the local church, the context for a service to mark the start of the ministry is not always clear. It may happen at a national Baptist Assembly if the call is to a denominational post, or at an Association gathering if the ministry is to be exercised in the Association. A College principal or tutor may be inducted at the College or in a local church associated with it. It may take the form of a traditional service of worship focusing on that one act. Alternatively, it may occupy a short time in the midst of other expressions of the life and work of the calling body. On some occasions a service of commissioning is held in the person's home church.

Whatever the context of such a service it will be important to explain fully the true nature of the new office. Representatives of the calling body should participate in order to emphasize that all ministry is fundamentally concerned with a calling and not only with an appointment. Ecumenical participation should be visible in order to emphasize that, as Baptists, we are but one part of the whole body of Christ, working together for his kingdom.

Below are suggestions for types of promises that may be used on various occasions. Firstly, promises for an induction service; secondly, promises for an affirmation of call (which may be necessary if an assembly or other such gathering can only meet some months after an appointment has been taken up); and thirdly, promises for an act of commissioning to a wider ministry by a local church.

PROMISES FOR AN ACT OF INDUCTION

LEADER TO THE PERSON CALLED TO WIDER
MINISTRY Do you believe in one God, Father,
Son, and Holy Spirit, and do you confess Jesus
Christ as your Saviour and Lord?

RESPONSE I do.

LEADER The apostle Paul spoke of his own self-
discipline: '. . . lest after preaching to others I
myself should be disqualified.' ——, in all your
tasks will you guard well your own true
discipleship and your joyful obedience to our
Lord and Saviour Jesus Christ?

RESPONSE By the grace of God I will.

LEADER Paul said to the elders at Ephesus, 'You
yourselves know how I lived among you, serving
the Lord with all humility and with tears. I did
not shrink from declaring to you the whole
counsel of God.' ——, by the grace of God will
you endeavour to exercise your ministry with
courage and commitment?

RESPONSE I will, the Lord helping me.

LEADER Paul also wrote of the demands of his wide
ministry, 'Apart from other things there is the
daily pressure upon me of my anxiety for all the
churches. Who is weak and I am not weak? Who
is made to fall and I am not indignant?' ——, your
special responsibility is to be . . . (*succinct
explanation of new role*). For the sake of Christ,
will you give yourself to the demands of such
service?

RESPONSE God giving me strength, I do so promise.

LEADER May God, who gives you the will to fulfil your ministry, grant you the grace to keep your vows.

LEADER TO THE MEMBERS OF THE CALLING BODY The apostle wrote, 'We beg you to acknowledge those who are working so hard among you and who in the Lord's fellowship are your leaders and counsellors. Hold them in the highest possible esteem and affection for the work they do.' If you are willing, in that spirit to receive —— now as your ——, I ask you to respond joyfully to the question I now ask you.
Do you acknowledge and receive —— as your ——, pledging *him/her* your affection, honour, and support in the Lord?

RESPONSE We do.

PROMISES FOR AN AFFIRMATION OF CALL

LEADER Brothers and sisters in Christ, I present to you —— who has been called through —— (*the name of appointing committee*) to work among us as ——. Today, we together welcome *him/her* to this role, affirming that we believe that it is God's will that *he/she* should work with us, and pledging ourselves to play our part in supporting and co-operating with *him/her*.

LEADER TO THE PERSON CALLED ——, do you believe in one God, Father, Son, and Holy Spirit, and do you confess Jesus Christ as your Saviour and Lord?

RESPONSE I do.

LEADER Do you believe that God has called you to this new step in ministry?

RESPONSE I do.

LEADER Do you believe that he who calls you to the task is also equipping you for it?

RESPONSE I do.

LEADER Do you today publicly acknowledge your commitment to work together with all those represented here for the greater glory of God? *(Details about the appointment may be added here)*

RESPONSE I do.

LEADER TO THE REPRESENTATIVES OF THE CALLING BODY
Do you believe that God has set —— apart to work with us and among us as ——, and do you believe that *he/she* is particularly gifted to serve us in this way?

RESPONSE We do.

LEADER Do you, on behalf of all those whom you represent by your presence here, pledge your willingness to work with —— and to support and encourage *him/her* as *he/she* exercises *his/her* ministry among us?

RESPONSE We do.

PROMISES FOR AN ACT OF COMMISSIONING

LEADER TO THE PERSON BEING COMMISSIONED
Do you believe in one God, Father, Son, and Holy Spirit, and do you confess Jesus Christ as your Saviour and Lord?

RESPONSE I do.

LEADER Paul said, 'In the presence of God and of

Christ Jesus, . . . I give you this charge: Preach the Word; be prepared in season and out of season; correct, rebuke, and encourage . . .; endure hardship . . .; discharge all the duties of your ministry.'

From 2 Timothy 4: 1–5

——, in your new appointment will you endeavour to fulfil this charge?

RESPONSE I will.

LEADER Paul also said, 'It was he [Christ] who gave some to be apostles, some to be prophets, some to be evangelists, and some to be pastors and teachers, to prepare God's people for works of service, so that the body of Christ may be built up until we all reach unity in the faith and in the knowledge of the Son of God and become mature, attaining to the whole measure of the fulness of Christ.'

Ephesians 4: 11–13

My *sister/brother*, will you see your task within the setting of all the ministries Christ has given to his Church, always making it your aim to build up the several parts into the one body of Christ?

RESPONSE I will.

LEADER TO THE MEMBERS OF THE SENDING CHURCH
Luke records that the Holy Spirit told the church at Antioch to set apart for him Barnabas and Saul. So after they had fasted and prayed they placed their hands upon them and sent them off. Do you believe that it is of the Holy Spirit that you should release your *pastor/sister/brother* for this wider ministry?

RESPONSE We do.

LEADER Is it your will that those who are
representatives among us should lay our hands
upon —— in commissioning and blessing?

RESPONSE It is.

LEADER Do you promise to remember *him/her* in
prayer and to support *him/her* as *he/she*
undertakes this wider ministry?

RESPONSE We do.

LEADER Let all the visitors present with us regard
themselves as representatives of the wider family
to which —— now goes, and stand with us for
this commissioning.

*The laying on of hands should now take place with
prayer, in accordance with the guidance given on
previous pages of this section.*

Ministry Overseas

A valedictory or commissioning service is usually held before a new missionary goes abroad for the first time. This is a time to underline the call of God to the new missionary (or missionaries) and for those present to surround them with love and prayer.

When a missionary couple has children whose lives will be greatly affected by this new step, it is important that each of the family is named and feels that they too will be supported by prayer.

Below is offered a pattern for an act of commissioning which may be the main focus of the worship or be incorporated in another act of worship. The singular is used throughout, but where a couple is involved the plural should of course be used.

The presiding leader should be a person who has had pastoral oversight of the missionary, preferably within the context of the local church.

Suitable scripture readings: Joshua 1: 1–9; Isaiah 6: 1–8; 42: 1–8; 49: 1–7; 60: 1–7; 61: 1–4; Jeremiah 1: 1–10; Matthew 9: 35–10: 16; 28: 18–20; Luke 10: 1–12; John 20: 19–23; Acts 1: 1–11; 13: 1–5; 16: 6–10; Romans 10: 1–17; 2 Corinthians 5: 11–21.

PATTERN FOR AN ACT OF COMMISSIONING

Introduction

An outline of the service may be given, extempore or as follows:

We have come together today to give thanks to God that he has chosen and set apart —— to work in

partnership with his church in ——. We come believing
that *he/she* is taking a step of obedience, and wishing
to surround *him/her* with our love and prayers as
he/she prepares to go.

The Call

*Here a representative of the sending body, or, if
possible, of the church or receiving body to which the
missionary is going, should outline what this new work
will entail. This may be done by words alone or by
imaginative use of visual resources.*

Hearing the Call

*Here the new missionary gives testimony to the way in
which he or she came to believe he or she was called by
God.*

Questions *to the missionary*

LEADER Do you believe in one God, Father, Son, and
Holy Spirit, and do you confess Jesus Christ as
your Saviour and Lord?

MISSIONARY I do.

LEADER Do you believe that Jesus Christ calls you and
all people everywhere with the words 'Follow
me'? Do you believe that at this time to be
obedient to the call of God you should work with
—— in ——?

MISSIONARY I do.

LEADER Jesus told his followers, 'Go to all peoples
everywhere and make them my disciples.' In your
ministry will you seek to ensure that the gospel of
Jesus Christ is proclaimed and demonstrated in

such a way that many may hear and understand his good news for them?

MISSIONARY I will.

LEADER You have heard God's call. Will you continue to listen to him speaking to you through people of a different language and a different culture?

MISSIONARY I will.

LEADER You have opened yourself to God. Do you believe that he has prepared you to go to —— to work in partnership with others? Do you go willing to give and to receive, to teach and to be taught?

MISSIONARY I do.

LEADER You have committed yourself to share Christ with others. Do you now recommit your life to him? Do you promise to make time for prayer, for reading of the scriptures, and for reflection, that all that you do may be firmly rooted in the love and knowledge of our Lord Jesus Christ?

MISSIONARY I do.

LEADER TO REPRESENTATIVE OF SENDING OR RECEIVING BODY ——, you represent —— here. It has been your task to test the call of —— and to help prepare *him/her* for the new work to which *he/she* now goes. Do you feel satisfied that ——'s departure for —— is within the will of God and do you believe that *he/she* is ready for this step of faith?

REPRESENTATIVE I do.

LEADER *to the congregation* You have come together to express your belief that —— is called to work in

——. You have come to express your good wishes and prayers as *he/she* prepares to leave. Do you commit yourselves to continue to pray for ——, to support *him/her/this family* and to express that prayer and support in practical ways?

CONGREGATION We do.

LEADER You send —— to —— in love. We can each learn much from our brothers and sisters in Christ in ——. Are you willing for your lives to be enriched by the strengthening of the bonds of Christian love which ——'s departure represents?

CONGREGATION We are.

Prayers for the missionary or missionary family, for their extended family and close friends, for the work to which they go and their future colleagues, and for all present.

These prayers may be extempore or as follows, and may be led by different people.

Our Father, we pray for —— (*name all directly affected*). We know that you call no one to a task that is beyond them and, confident of this, we pray for ——.
In all the things that they find hard about this new work, may they know that you are with them and will not fail them. When times are good, may they continue to be aware of the presence of your Spirit, enlivening and enhancing all love and laughter.

LEADER Lord of all the world

CONGREGATION Bless your children, we pray.

LEADER We pray for the family and friends of ——. As

they face the loss of separation, may they too
know your peace that passes all understanding.

LEADER Lord of all the world

CONGREGATION Bless your children, we pray.

LEADER Our Father, we give you thanks for all that is
being done in your name in ——.
As —— joins those at work there, may the period
of transition be smooth, and trust and
understanding quickly grow.

LEADER Lord of all the world

CONGREGATION Bless your children, we pray.

LEADER Our Father, we pray for ourselves that we may
not stop our ears to your continuing call. Help us
not to be too frightened to listen for new
challenges and, when we have listened, help us
dare to respond.

LEADER Lord of all the world

CONGREGATION Bless your children, we pray.

At the end of the service

LEADER AND CONGREGATION ——, go in peace, love
and serve the Lord, rejoicing in the power of the
Holy Spirit.

MISSIONARY In the name of Christ, Amen.

The Grace is said together.

For use, if desired, in the second pattern of ordination on page 188.

Baptist Union of Great Britain

Declaration of Principle

The basis of this Union is:

1. That our Lord and Saviour Jesus Christ, God manifest in the flesh, is the sole and absolute authority in all matters pertaining to faith and practice, as revealed in the Holy Scriptures, and that each church has liberty, under the guidance of the Holy Spirit, to interpret and administer His laws.

2. That Christian Baptism is the immersion in water into the name of the Father, the Son, and the Holy Ghost, of those who have professed repentance towards God and faith in our Lord Jesus Christ who 'died for our sins according to the Scriptures; was buried, and rose again the third day'.

3. That it is the duty of every disciple to bear personal witness to the Gospel of Jesus Christ, and to take part in the evangelization of the world.

THE LIFE OF THE CHURCH

In this section material is provided for significant occasions in the life of the local church. It is assumed that such occasions will be set within fuller services planned as each church decides. Therefore complete patterns of worship are not included here. The occasions covered are:

The formation of a church.

Laying a foundation stone.

Opening a new church building.

Inside the church building: the dedication of furnishings such as communion table, lectern etc.

The church meeting.

The church gathering for prayer.

A service of healing.

The Formation of a Church

Such a significant moment should always be marked by the presence of the wider Christian community. The General Superintendent, representatives of the local Baptist Association, and guests from other branches of the Christian Church and of the civic community should be invited. Where there is an ecumenical situation, with a shared building or an ecumenical fellowship, the service should be planned in co-operation with the other participants.

When the congregation is gathered together, it is appropriate that the believers who are to form the new church should sit together at the front.

The act of covenanting together should come as the climax of a service of worship and the preaching of God's Word.

The Minister, Church Secretary, or another representative of the new church tells of the steps that led to the formation of this new church, laying special emphasis on why the people believe it is the will of the Lord Jesus Christ to establish his Church in this place.

Act of Covenanting

THE GENERAL SUPERINTENDENT We have come together today in the name of our Lord Jesus Christ so that you may make a covenant with the Lord and with each other, and so become a fully constituted church of believers.

There are four requirements of all who enter into this covenant:

- faith in the Lord Jesus Christ;
- mutual love within the fellowship;
- a willingness to obey Christ's great commission;
- a commitment to the wider fellowship of God's people, and a desire to work with others as far as is possible.

The members of the new church stand.

LEADER As believers who are to form the —— Church, do you re-affirm your faith in the One God, Father, Son, and Holy Spirit, knowing that you

have been born again into the Body of Christ by
the Holy Spirit?

PEOPLE We do.

LEADER Jesus said: 'I give you a new commandment:
love one another; as I have loved you, so you are
to love one another. If there is this love among
you, then everyone will know that you are my
disciples.'

John 13: 34–35

Will you now re-affirm your mutual love and
acceptance of one another by giving 'The
Peace' to each other?

*The new members share the Peace (see The
Lord's Supper pp. 83–4.)*

LEADER The apostle Paul writes: 'You are fellow-
citizens with God's people, members of God's
household. You are built upon the foundation laid
by the apostles and prophets, and Christ Jesus
himself is the foundation stone. In him the whole
building is bonded together.'

Ephesians 2: 19–21a

LEADER We now invite representatives of the Baptist
community and the wider Church to greet you.

*The representatives give the right hand of
fellowship to the Minister and Church
Secretary.*

The new members stand and say together:

Trusting in Jesus Christ as Saviour, and confessing him
as Lord, we covenant together to walk with God, in all
his ways made known or to be made known, and in all
the responsibilities and privileges of church fellowship

and worship, service, and witness; in the name of the Father, and of the Son, and of the Holy Spirit.

As an act of unity, the entire congregation should be asked to stand, and a prayer be offered, which may either be extempore or based on the following pattern.

LEADER We dedicate this fellowship to live to the glory of the everlasting God, Father, Son, and Holy Spirit.

Father, we praise you that you made the whole earth to shine with your glory.
Lord Jesus, we praise you that you lived among us, and we saw your glory, that you were lifted up on the Cross for us, raised from death, and exalted to heaven.
Holy Spirit, we praise you that on the day of Pentecost you established Christ's Church and have built it on the foundation of the apostles and prophets, with Christ Jesus as its chief corner-stone.

Now we pray for this new fellowship, that your people may be obedient to the vision you have given them. May they be:
a witnessing church, where Jesus Christ is proclaimed as Saviour and Lord;
a teaching church, their mind formed by the Apostolic faith;
a loving church, where forgiveness and mutual care prevail;
an obedient church, where Christ alone is Head;
a serving church, overflowing in care and concern for all who are in need;

a visionary church, ever seeking to discern the signs of the Spirit's action in the world.

As this church goes on in fellowship with the Association, the Union, and the whole Church of Christ, we pray that we may support and encourage one another, and grow together in the unity of the Spirit; through Jesus Christ our Lord.

The members of the new church may now come forward and sign the church roll.

Hymn

The Lord's Supper

Hymn

Dismissal and Benediction

Laying a Foundation Stone

As with the Formation of a Church, it is important to include the wider Christian fellowship. Please refer to the introduction to that section. Where the building is to be shared with other Christians, or is to be for an ecumenical fellowship, many other factors will be involved in the preparation of the order of service. The builder and/or architect should be invited to be present.

The person presiding welcomes everybody.

A representative of the local church gives a statement telling of all the circumstances that led to the decision to build, and affirming the conviction that this action is in obedience to the leading of God's Spirit.

The presiding minister/leader invites the person appointed to lay the stone, assisted by the builder.

The leader then says:

In the name of Almighty God, the Father, the Son, and the Holy Spirit:
we lay this foundation stone of —— Church.

Unless the Lord builds the house, its builders will have toiled in vain.
Psalm 127: 1

There can be no other foundation beyond that which is already laid; I mean Jesus Christ himself.
1 Corinthians 3: 11

To God be all the glory; through Jesus Christ our Lord.

The prayer of dedication is offered, which may be either extempore or based on the example below.

Almighty and ever present God, you are in every part of your creation, but in your wisdom you have given us special places where your presence may be more readily found by our restless spirits.
So we come to ask, for the house of prayer that will rise in this place, the consecration of your presence and Spirit.
We pray that through the influence of the worship and service of this place, every place, every day, and every activity may be more and more felt to be sacred, and the whole earth be none other but the house of God and the gate of heaven.

The Doxology may be sung.

Prayers for the Future

For the worship and teaching—perhaps given by a deacon or member. For the witness to the gospel—by a representative of the wider Church. For service within the community—by a church member.

A Hymn may be sung

Dismissal and Benediction

Opening a New Church Building

As with the Formation of a Church and Laying a Foundation Stone, the wider Christian community will have a place in this service. The ecumenical considerations referred to above will also apply.

The Entrance

If possible the congregation may be gathered outside the closed doors of the church. Otherwise the congregation may assemble inside the church building and the doors be locked two minutes before the service is due to begin. Those involved in the opening ceremony remain outside. Sound relay/amplification should be provided as necessary.

> *The presiding minister invites the builder to hand the key to the person chosen to perform the opening.*
>
> *The door is unlocked.*
>
> *The party (with the congregation) enter and take their places.*

A Hymn may be sung as the party enters.

When all are ready, the presiding minister says:

Lift up your heads, you gates,
lift yourselves up, you everlasting doors,
that the king of glory may come in.   *Psalm 24: 7*

Enter his gates with thanksgiving
and his courts with praise.
Give thanks to him and bless his name;
for the Lord is good and his love is everlasting.
                                        Psalm 100: 4–5a

Let us pray:

Our Father, make the door of this house we have
raised wide enough to receive all who need human love
and fellowship and your fatherly care; and narrow
enough to shut out all envy, pride, and hate.
Make its threshold smooth enough to be no stumbling-
block to little children, the weak or the wandering, but
rugged enough and strong enough to turn back the
tempter's power.
God, make the door of this house the gateway to your
eternal kingdom; through Jesus Christ our Lord.

The Doxology may be sung.

Service of Worship

Hymn of Praise

Prayer

Reading of Scripture

> *Suitable readings are: 1 Kings 8: 22–30;*
> *1 Chronicles 29: 10–18; Psalms 24; 84; 122;*
> *Matthew 16: 13–20; 1 Corinthians 3: 10–17;*
> *Ephesians 2: 11–22; 3: 14–21; 1 Peter 2: 4–10.*

Sermon

Hymn

> *All stand. The leader says:*

In the name of the Lord Jesus Christ we do this.
To the glory of God the Father, who has called us by
his grace:
To the glory of the Son, who loves us and gave himself
for us:
And to the glory of the Holy Spirit, who brings us to
the light, gives us strength, and is the source of our
love:
We dedicate this church building.

May worship and prayer be offered, the gospel be
preached, and the sacraments of the Lord's Supper and
Baptism be celebrated, so that faith may be
strengthened, hope made brighter, and love made
deeper.
May the gospel be demonstrated in fellowship and
service.
May many come to know the Lord, and be built up,
and sustained by their faith.

May the young find guidance, may family life be
enriched, may the sick and the sad find comfort
and help.

We remember that Jesus prayed that his disciples might
be one.

May we ever keep in mind that we are one small
branch of a world family.

May we seek to share with God's people everywhere in
proclaiming by word and action the gospel of the
Kingdom of God.

And finally, as the people who will serve God in this
place, we dedicate again our lives and our gifts to him.

Now with God's people everywhere we join to say:

Our Father . . .

Hymn

Dismissal and Benediction

Inside the Church Building

Dedication of furnishings etc.

Where a NEW BUILDING *is being opened, it may be
thought fitting to include the dedication of various
furnishings in the opening ceremony. Otherwise, they
may be considered part of the total dedication and not
treated separately. Alternatively, it may be felt suitable
to dedicate them the following Sunday—or when they
are first used (in the case of a Baptistry or Communion
Table).*

Baptists have not generally placed much emphasis

upon sacred objects, places, and ceremonies. Their free tradition pays more attention to the inward, spiritual consciousness of the worshippers. It is appropriate, therefore, to ask the question: What is the purpose of the dedication of church furnishings? Three suggestions can be offered.

(1) It may be seen as the setting aside of objects for special use. The thing dedicated will be a thing apart, e.g. the Table is not any table to be used for modelling and painting during the week.

(2) Its purpose may be that of praying for the ministry that will be associated with it.

(3) It may be a recognition that the God who fills all creation and may manifest himself in any part of it, chooses particular places where he discloses himself in special ways.

There is also a growing awareness that worship is to be the worship of the whole person—body, mind, and spirit. There is, therefore, a growing recognition of the place of the visual—banners, symbols, sacred dance and mime, the careful use of ritual and gesture—and of the importance of material objects such as Communion Tables, vessels, lecterns etc.

A COMMUNION TABLE

This may take place on a Sunday when the Lord's Supper is to be celebrated. At the appropriate part of the service, the minister or leader approaches the table.

LEADER We are here to dedicate this Table which will be used for the celebration of the ordinance of the Lord's Supper. Let us hear the word of scripture.

Luke 22: 7–13; 1 Corinthians 10: 16–17

> *Prayer is then offered.*

> *The deacons bring forward the communion plate and vessels and set the table. Two chosen members of the congregation bring forward a cup and a loaf.*

LEADER The Table of the Lord is set. Let us prepare ourselves. Let us greet one another as a sign of our oneness in Christ.

> *Then follows the observance of the Lord's Supper.*

A LECTERN

This may take place during a Sunday service of worship. At the point of the service where scripture is to be read, the leader introduces the act of dedication, giving any relevant details, e.g. if it is a gift or memorial, and speaks of the importance of the reading of the Word in Christian worship.

> *The Bible is carried in and opened.*

LEADER Let us hear the word of scripture.

> *A selection from the following or other appropriate verses may be read.*

Psalms 1; 105; 119; Isaiah 40: 6b–8; 55: 8–11; Matthew 7: 24–27; Luke 21: 33; 2 Timothy 3: 16–17.

> *Prayer is then offered.*

> *The scripture for the day is then read.*

A PULPIT

This may take place during a Sunday service of worship. The service may be conducted from a lectern or the Communion Table. After the scripture reading, the leader introduces the act of dedication, giving any relevant details, e.g. if it is a gift or memorial, and speaks of the importance of the preaching of the Word in Christian worship.

LEADER Let us hear the word of scripture.

A selection of the following or other appropriate verses may be read.

Isaiah 52: 7–10; John 12: 21; 1 Corinthians 2: 1–10; 2 Timothy 4: 1–5.

Prayer is then offered.

A BAPTISTRY

Where possible, it is fitting that this should take place when persons are to be baptized. If this is not convenient, it is important to have the baptistry filled with water and prepared as for a baptism.

At an appropriate part of the service the leader introduces the act of dedication, giving any relevant details, e.g. if it is a gift or memorial, speaks of the importance of the Baptism of Believers, and sets out its meaning. Material from the Baptismal Service may be used here.

LEADER Let us hear the word of scripture.

Matthew 28: 18–20; Romans 6: 4.

Prayer is then offered.

Where there is to be a baptism, the service proceeds.

The Church Meeting

The Church Meeting is an act of communal discipleship, seeking the mind of Christ in prayer. It begins with worship which needs to be prepared with great care and sensitivity. The purpose of this worship is adoration, praise, and prayer for the Holy Spirit's inspiration and guidance. In this way the life of the community and the discussion that will follow is set in its true light. It is a lifting of hearts and minds that have for many hours in the day been engaged in this world, so that they may renew their sense of God and his lordship over his people. Wherever possible, it is good for the deacons or elders to lead this on a rota basis.

Call to Worship

Bible Reading

Brief Address

Prayer

Hymn/Song

It is appropriate to pause for prayer during the course of the meeting, using such words as:

Father, we seek the guidance of your Holy Spirit
in the business that is before us.
In planning for the future, give us vision;

In matters of finance, give us responsibility;
In dealing with people, give us love.
Help us in all things to honour your name, to advance
your kingdom, and to carry out your will; through
Jesus Christ our Lord.

The Church Gathering for Prayer

*The regular meeting for prayer is an essential part of
the church's life. By this regular commitment to prayer,
the church makes a statement about its identity as a
people obedient to its Head, Jesus Christ, our Lord.
The purpose of the meeting is prayer—not bible study.
Here the church listens, lays its life before God,
expresses its need, perplexities, differences, and
conflicts, and offers intercessions for every aspect of its
continuing life and ministry. Below is a suggested
outline for a meeting lasting one hour. It is good to
plan it well with a group of people, and to use visual
aids in order to seek variety and freshness.*

Hymn/Song

Simple Prayer of Approach

Brief Comment *on some aspect of prayer*

Prayers of Thanksgiving *for the past few weeks of the
church's life*

Hymn/Song

Prayers, *in small groups, for the next few weeks of the
church's life: e.g. the services, youth work, Sunday
School, any special events*

Hymn/Song
> *Return to larger grouping*

Special Subject *for the evening, e.g. One World Week, missionary work, youth work, the worship of the church, people or items in the news*

Closing Hymn/Song

A Service of Healing

Introduction

The ministry of healing may take place in a variety of ways.

1. Some churches occasionally include the laying on of hands in a Sunday service or towards the close of the Lord's Supper.

2. Sometimes a short service is held in the home of a sick person, with members of the family and a few representatives of the church present. This should normally be at the request of the sick person or family in accordance with the scriptural teaching in James 5: 14.

3. On occasions there may be a request for the ministry of healing by a patient in hospital. It is then wise to consult with the hospital staff about the arrangements and to ensure that prayer for them and for other patients is included.

4. In some churches it is the custom to hold a healing service once a month on a weekday. Others have a regular time for prayers for the sick, either in a special meeting or in small groups at church or at home.

Whatever pattern is adopted, it is important that clear teaching is given within the church fellowship so that the nature and purpose of the ministry may be understood and false expectations are not aroused. Ideally the Church Meeting should be given opportunity to affirm this ministry as part of the normal life of the church. It will then be seen to be the church's ministry and not that of an individual, even though he or she may be spiritually gifted for such a ministry. Scriptural teaching makes clear that all spiritual gifts are to be exercised within the life of the whole Body (1 Corinthians 12).

Healing was undoubtedly part of the total ministry of Jesus. As the risen Lord who is 'the same yesterday, today, and for ever', he continues his healing work now. He commissioned his disciples to preach, teach, and heal. All three activities were to be signs of the Kingdom of God. The New Testament gives many examples of the way in which healing was a normal part of Christian ministry. The Church today is given the same three-fold commission. Such a conviction is essential to the ministry of healing.

It is also important to make clear that God is the healer, according to his sovereign will. He heals through doctors and nurses, through medicine, surgery, and psychiatry, through faith and prayer, and through the loving fellowship and pastoral care of the Church. He uses all these channels. The Church's ministry is never in place of doctors or in rivalry with them, but alongside them, supporting them prayerfully, and going on when they seem to have reached the limits of their ability. It is important to stress that God is not limited by the limits of human knowledge and skill.

Certain features are important in the ministry of healing:

Worship which focuses attention primarily on God, the Father, Son, and Holy Spirit.

Proclamation of the Word of God, however briefly.

Prayers of self-emptying, confession, and repentance, so that all barriers to wholeness are removed.

Prayer for healing in which the sick person is lifted up to God, concentrating on the divine love, peace, power, and compassion, not on symptoms of disease.

The laying on of hands as a sign of identification with the sick person, as a symbol of blessing, and as a means which God can use to release the power of the Holy Spirit into our lives.

In some situations anointing with oil is practised. Olive oil would normally be used.

A stress on wholeness in such terms as the words of Jesus in John 10: 10. The emphasis should be on God's perfect will for each of his children, and on his unfailing love from which nothing in life or death can separate us.

A Pattern of Service

The minister or leader should introduce the service with such words as these:

We have come together because we believe that our wholeness of spirit, mind, and body, is truly God's will. Our Lord Jesus Christ has commanded his Church to continue his healing ministry, and we believe that he is present among us now.

We come, then, believing that all of us will receive his blessing, which will affect our lives in different ways. In many cases there will be recovery or improvement of health. For some this will happen quickly, for others it may take longer. Some may experience inner healing of mind and spirit.

Even if there are no apparent signs of physical healing, let us not imagine that it is because of our lack of faith or worthiness. We come to place ourselves in the Lord's hands, to surrender to his purpose and will for us. Then we shall always receive a blessing, whether we are conscious of any changes in ourselves or not.

The laying on of hands is primarily a ministry to the human spirit as we pray for the indwelling of the Holy Spirit at the centre of our being.

Scripture Sentences

The Lord is near. Do not be anxious about anything, but in everything, by prayer and petition, with thanksgiving, present your requests to God. And the peace of God, which transcends all understanding, will guard your hearts and your minds in Christ Jesus.

Philippians 4: 5b, 6–7

Great is the Lord, and greatly to be praised, and his greatness is unsearchable. *Psalm 145: 3*

Be still before the Lord, and wait patiently for him.

Psalm 37: 7

Where two or three meet together in my name, I am there among them.   *Matthew 18: 20*

Come to me, all who are weary and whose load is heavy; I will give you rest.   *Matthew 11: 28*

Hymn

Prayer of Adoration

Prayer of Confession, Followed by Declaration of Forgiveness

Scripture Reading

Meditation on the Scripture

Hymn

> *An invitation to come forward may be given at this point, in words such as the following:*

During the singing you are invited to come forward to receive the laying on of hands for yourself or for another, for healing of mind, body, and spirit, forgiveness of sin, help in facing personal problems, or assurance of salvation in Christ.
Come with the assurance that all of us will be surrounding you in love and prayer.

> *If any come forward without their particular need being known to the minister or leader, they may briefly indicate it during the singing.*

Prayer of Preparation

> *This will include thanksgiving for the love of God, the healing ministry of Christ, the promise of healing today, and any experiences of healing known to the*

*group from recent experience. Then may follow a time
of guided silence, when the congregation are invited to
seek closer communion with God, and confidence in his
presence and work among them.*

The Laying On of Hands

> *This may be accompanied by extempore prayer or
> as follows:*

Lord, you can do all things. Take —— as *he/she* is, and
make *him/her* what you want *him/her* to be.

> *Or:*

——, may the Holy Spirit come upon you afresh,
entering into your spirit, your mind, and your body,
bringing you the renewal and healing that is his will.

> *The minister or leader may then say:*

Jesus said, 'Your faith has made you well; go in peace,
and be healed of your disease.'   *Mark 5: 34*

Intercessions

> *Prayer for any known to the fellowship who are ill or
> in any kind of need;
> prayer for those who work in hospitals;
> prayer for those who care for the sick and infirm in
> their own homes;
> prayer for those in anxiety for friends or loved ones.*

Set free, O Lord, the souls of your servants from all
restlessness and anxiety; give them that peace and
power which flows from you, and keep them in all
perplexities and distresses, in all griefs and grievances,
from any fear or faithlessness, that so upheld by your

strength and stayed on the rock of your faithfulness,
through storm and stress they may abide in you.

Hymn

Prayer

Father, we abandon ourselves into your hands; do with
us what you will, and we shall give you praise.
Let only your will be done in us, and in all your
creatures.
Into your hands we commend our spirit, with the love
of our hearts, with boundless confidence and certainty
of hope, because you are our Father.

Benediction

READINGS THROUGH THE YEAR

This is a new lectionary of bible readings, spread over four years and prepared by the Joint Liturgical Group. Apart from providing more readings and less repetition over a four-year period, each year concentrates on a single Gospel, thus encouraging expository preaching.

To synchronize use of the lectionary with other Christians, it is suggested that the ninth Sunday before Christmas in Year A should begin towards the end of 1992 and subsequent timings be calculated from that point.

If all the lessons are not read, the Old Testament should always be read on the Sundays before Christmas, the Gospel from Christmas Day to the 6th after Easter (the Sunday after Ascension Day), and the Epistle or equivalent New Testament lesson from Pentecost to the Last Sunday after Pentecost. Verses in brackets may be omitted.

Year A	Year B	Year C	Year D
9th Sunday before Christmas			
Prov 8.1, 22–31	Gen 2.4b–9, 15–25	Job 38.1–18	Gen 1.1–5, 24–31a
Rev 21.1–4, 22–27	Rev 4.1–11	Acts 14.8–17	Col 1.15–20
Mt 10.28–33	Mk 10.2–12	Lk 12.13–31	Jn 1.1–14
8th Sunday before Christmas			
Isa 44.6–17	Gen 4.1–10	Gen 9.8–17	Gen 3.1–15
Rom 3.21–28	1 Jn 3.9–18	Rom 5.12–21	Rom 7.7–13
Mt 23.25–36	Mk 7.14–23	Lk 11.33–41	Jn 3.13–21
7th Sunday before Christmas			
Gen 13.1–18	Gen 15.1–18	Gen 18.1–16	Gen 12.1–9
Gal 3.1–14	Jas 2.14–26	Rom 9.1–9	Rom 4.13–25
Mt 3.7–12	Mk 12.18–27	Lk 3.1–14	Jn 8.51–59

Year A	Year B	Year C	Year D

6th Sunday before Christmas

Deut 18.15–22	Exod 6.2–13	Exod 3.1–15	Exod 2.1–10
Acts 3.11–26	Heb 11.17–29	Heb 8.1–13	Heb 3.1–6
Mt 5.38–48	Mk 13.5–13	Lk 20.27–40	Jn 6.27–35

5th Sunday before Christmas

Micah 2.12–13	1 Sam 16.1–13	2 Sam 5.1–5	Jer 23.1–6
Rev 19.11–16	1 Tim 1.12–17	1 Cor 15.20–28	Rev 1.4–8
Mt 25.31–46	Mk 10.17–31	Lk 23.35–43	Jn 18.33–40

4th Sunday before Christmas: Advent Sunday

Isa 2.1–5	Isa 51.4–11	Jer 33.14–16	Isa 52.1–10
Rom 13.8–14	1 Thess 5.1–11	Jas 5.1–11	Rom 11.13–24
Mt 24.36–44	Mk 13.21–37	Lk 21.25–36	Jn 7.25–31

3rd Sunday before Christmas: Advent 2

Isa 59.12–20	Jer 36.1–10	Isa 55.1–11	1 Kings 22.(1–5) 6–17
Rom 16.25–27	2 Tim 3.14–4.8	Rom 15.4–13	2 Pet 1.19–2.3
Mt 13.53–58	Mk 7.1–13	Lk 4.14–21	Jn 5.36–47

2nd Sunday before Christmas: Advent 3

Judg 13.2–14	Isa 40.1–11	Zeph 3.14–18	Mal 4.1–6
Phil 4.4–9	2 Pet 3.8–14	1 Thess 5.16–24	1 Cor 4.1–5
Mt 11.2–19	Mk 1.1–8	Lk 1.5–25	Jn 1.19–28

Sunday next before Christmas: Advent 4

Isa 7.10–14	1 Sam 2.1–10	Isa 11.1–10	Zech 2.10–13
Rev 11.19–12.6	Rom 1.1–7	1 Cor 1.26–31	Heb 10.1–10
Mt 1.18–23	Lk 1.39–56	Lk 1.26–38a	Lk 1.57–66

**On this Sunday Lk 1.68–79 may well be used as a canticle

Year A	Year B	Year C	Year D
Christmas midnight			
Micah 5.2–4	Isa 9.2, 6–7	Isa 45.22–25	Isa 7.10–14
Titus 2.11–15	Titus 3.4–7	Phil 2.1–13	Heb 1.1–6
Lk 2.1–20	Lk 2.1–20	Jn 1.1–14	Lk 2.1–20
Christmas Day			
Isa 9.2, 6–7	Isa 52.7–14	Micah 5.2–4	Isa 62.6–7, 10–12
1 Jn 4.7–14	Heb 1.1–6	Titus 2.11–15	Titus 3.4–7
Jn 1.1–14	Jn 1.1–14	Lk 2.1–20	Jn 1.1–14
1st Sunday after Christmas			
Isa 60.1–6	Isa 49.7–13	Isa 61.1–11	Isa 11.1–10
Eph 3.1–12	Rev 21.22–22.5	1 Jn 1.1–2.2	Gal 3.26–4.7
Mt 2.1–12	Mt 2.1–12	Mt 2.1–12	Mt 2.1–12

**Where this Sunday falls on 30 December, the lessons for the 2nd Sunday after Christmas (C2) are read.

Year A	Year B	Year C	Year D
2nd Sunday after Christmas			
Jer 31.15–17	Zech 8.1–8	1 Sam 1.20–28	Isa 40.25–31
2 Cor 1.3–11	1 Thess 2.1–8	Rom 12.1–8	Col 1.1–14
Mt 2.13–23	Lk 2.41–52	Lk 2.21–40	Jn 1.14–18
Epiphany			
Isa 49.13–23	Isa 49.1–6	Isa 60.1–6	Isa 49.7–13
Rom 15.13–21	Gal 4.1–7	Eph 3.1–12	Rev 21.22–22.5
Mt 2.1–12	Mt 2.1–12	Mt 2.1–12	Mt 2.1–12
1st Sunday after Epiphany			
1 Sam 16.1–13a	Exod 14.15–22	Josh 3.1–17	Isa 42.1–9
Rom 6.12–23	1 Jn 5.6–9	Acts 10.34–48a	Eph 2.1–10
Mt 3.13–17	Mk 1.9–11	Lk 3.15–22	Jn 1.29–34

Year A	Year B	Year C	Year D
2nd Sunday after Epiphany			
Ezek 2.1–3.4	Jer 1.4–10	Exod 18.13–27	1 Sam 3.1–10
Rev 10.8–11	Acts 9.1–20	Acts 16.(6–10) 11–15	Gal 1.11–24
Mt 4.18–25	Mk 1.14–20	Lk 5.1–11	Jn 1.35–51
3rd Sunday after Epiphany			
Isa 9.1–4	Deut 30.11–15	Num 9.15–23	Exod 33.12–23
Rom 1.8–17	1 Pet 1.3–12	1 Cor 1.1–9	1 Jn 1.1–4
Mt 4.12–17	Mk 1.21–28	Lk 4.16–30	Jn 2.1–11
4th Sunday after Epiphany			
Gen 28.10–22	1 Chr 29.(1–5) 6–19	Hagg 2.1–9	1 Kings 8.22–30
Acts 7.44–50	1 Cor 6.12–20	2 Cor 6.14–7.1	1 Cor 3.10–17
Mt 21.12–16	Mk 1.40–45	Lk 21.1–9	Jn 2.13–25
5th Sunday after Epiphany			
Isa 6.(1–7) 8–12	2 Sam 12.1–13a	Jer 13.1–11	Judg 9.7–15
Rom 1.18–25	1 Pet 1.22–25	1 Cor 2.1–5	1 Cor 10.1–13
Mt 13.10–17	Mk 4.10–12, 21–34	Lk 5.33–39	Jn 12.37–50
6th Sunday after Epiphany			
1 Sam 21.1–6	Isa 1.10–17	Exod 20.8–11	Deut 5.12–15
Rom 2.1–11	Col 2.16–19	1 Cor 3.18–23	2 Cor 2.14–3.6
Mt 12.1–14	Mk 2.23–3.6	Lk 6.1–11	Jn 7.14–24
9th Sunday before Easter			
Isa 30.18–21	Prov 2.1–9	Prov 3.1–8	Job 22.12–28
1 Tim 4.(4–7a) 7b–16	1 Cor 2.6–10	1 Cor 4.8–16	2 Jn 1–13
Mt 5.(1–12) 17–20	Mk 4.1–9	Lk 8.4–15	Jn 8.21–36

Year A	Year B	Year C	Year D

8th Sunday before Easter

2 Kings 5.1–14 (15–19a)	2 Kings 4.18–37	Job 2.1–10	Job 23.1–10
2 Cor 12.1–10	Jas 5.13–16	Acts 3.1–10	Jas 1.2–5
Mt 15.21–31	Mk 2.1–12	Lk 5.12–26	Jn 5.1–18

7th Sunday before Easter

Isa 30.8–17	Jonah 1.1–17	Isa 41.8–16	Deut 8.1–6
Acts 12.1–17	Heb 2.1–4	Acts 28.1–6	Phil 4.10–20
Mt 14.22–36	Mk 4.35–41	Lk 9.10–17	Jn 6.1–15

Ash Wednesday

Joel 2.12–18	Isa 58.1–8	Amos 5.6–15	Exod 20.1–17
2 Tim 2.1–7	1 Cor 9.19–27	Jas 4.1–10	2 Cor 5.14–6.2
Mt 6.16–21	Mk 2.18–22	Lk 18.1–14	Mt 6.1–15

1st Sunday in Lent

Deut 30.15–20	Jer 31.27–34	Deut 6.10–17	Exod 17.3–7
Jas 1.12–18	Heb 2.10–18	Rom 10.8–13	Heb 4.12–16
Mt 4.1–11	Mk 1.12–15	Lk 4.1–13	Mt 4.1–11

2nd Sunday in Lent

Isa 35.1–10	Jer 2.1–13	Gen 6.11–22	2 Kings 6.8–17
1 Jn 3.1–10	Eph 6.10–20	1 Jn 4.1–6	Eph 5.6–14
Mt 12.22–32	Mk 3.19b–27	Lk 11.14–26	Jn 9.(1–12) 13–41

3rd Sunday in Lent

Job 1.1–12	Isa 48.1–8	Isa 63.7–14	Josh 24.14–24
1 Pet 4.12–19	2 Tim 1.8–14	2 Tim 2.8–13	Gal 2.11–21
Mt 16.13–28	Mk 8.27–33	Lk 9.18–27	Jn 6.60–71

Year A	Year B	Year C	Year D

4th Sunday in Lent

Exod 24.3–11	Exod 24.12–18	Exod 34.29–35	1 Sam 9.27–10.1, 6–7
2 Pet 1.16–19	2 Cor 4.1–6	2 Cor 3.4–18	2 Cor 1.15–22
Mt 17.1–13	Mk 9.2–10	Lk 9.28–36	Jn 12.1–8

**Where the Fourth Sunday in Lent is observed as Mothering Sunday, the following readings are offered:

Gen 21.8–21	1 Sam 1.9–20	Isa 66.5–13	Jer 31.15–20
Rom 16.1–7	Gal 4.21–5.1	1 Thess 2.1–8	Heb 11.1–2, 11–12
Mt 23.29–39	Mk 3.31–35	Lk 1.39–45 (46–55)	Lk 2.41–52

5th Sunday in Lent

Gen 25.29–34	Lam 3.(1–9) 18–33	Lam 1.1–14	Isa 63.1–9
Rom 8.1–11	Rom 5.1–11	Heb 5.1–10	Col 2.8–15
Mt 20.20–28	Mk 10.32–45	Lk 20.9–19	Jn 12.20–36

Palm Sunday

Zech 9.9(10)	Zech 9.9(10)	Zech 9.9(10)	Zech 9.9(10)
Mt 21.1–11	Mk 11.1–11	Lk 19.29–40 (41–44)	Jn 12.12–16
Lam 5.15–22	Isa 50.4–7	Isa 56.1–8	Gen 22.1–18
1 Cor 1.18–25	Phil 2.5–11	Heb 10.1–10	Heb 10.11–25
Mt (26.36–27.31) 27.32–54 (55–56)	Mk (14.32–15.20) 15.21–39 (40–41)	Lk (22.39–23.31) 23.32–49	Mt (26.36–27.31) 27.32–54 (55–56) or John 18.1–40

**On Palm Sunday and Good Friday provision is made, as is traditional, for reading the greater part of the passion narratives, but where these passages are not read in full, the earlier parts of the narratives may be read at evening services during Lent or on the Monday, Tuesday, and Wednesday of Holy Week.

Year A	Year B	Year C	Year D
Maundy Thursday			
Exod 24.3–8	Exod 12.1–8, 11–14	Gen 14.18–20	Jer 31.31–34
1 Cor 10.16–17	1 Cor 11.23–29	1 Cor 10.16–17	1 Cor 11.23–29
Mt 26.26–35	Mk 14.12–26	Lk 22.14–38	Jn 13.1–15
Good Friday			
Lam 2.15–19	Gen 22.1–18	Isa 52.13–53.12	Isa 50.4–9
Heb 10.11–25	Heb 4.14–16, 5.7–9	Heb 10.11–25	Col 1.18–23
John (18.1–19.16) 19.17–37	John (18.1–19.16) 19.17–37	John (18.1–19.16) 19.17–37	John (18.1–19.16) 19.17–37

**or Palm Sunday gospels may be read

Easter Day: first service

(Gen 1.1–5, 26–31)	(Gen. 3.8–13, 22–24)	(Gen 7.1–5, 10–18, 8.6–18, 9.8–13)	(Exod 4.27–5.1)
Exod 14.15–22 or 14.15–15.1	Exod 14.15–22 or 14.15–15.1	Exod 14.15–22 or 14.15–15.1	Exod 14.15–22 or 14.15–15.1
(Ezek 36.16–28)	(Isa 55.1–11)	(Isa 54.4–14)	(Deut 31.22–29)
Rom 6.3–11	Rom 6.3–11	Rom 6.3–11	Rom 6.3–11
Mt 28.1–10	Mk 16.1–8	Lk 24.1–11	Mt 28.1–10

**If the service includes a vigil, all the lessons should be read. If it is in the early morning, those in brackets should be omitted.

Easter Day: second service

Year A	Year B	Year C	Year D
Isa 12.1–6	Isa 42.10–16	Jer 31.1–6	Isa 55.1–11
Rev 1.12–18	1 Cor 15.1–11	1 Cor 15.12–20	1 Cor 5.7b–8
Jn 20.1–18	Jn 20.1–18	Jn 20.1–18	Jn 20.1–18

Year A	Year B	Year C	Year D

1st Sunday after Easter

Isa 65.17–25	Num 13.1–2, 17–33	2 Kings 7.1–16	Exod 15.1–11
Acts 13.26–31	2 Cor 4.7–18	Rev 19.6–9	1 Pet 1.3–9
Mt 28.11–15	John 20.19–31	Lk 24.13–35	Jn 20.19–31

2nd Sunday after Easter

1 Kings 17.(8–16) 17–24	Ezek 34.7–15	Isa 51.1–6	Isa 61.1–3
Col 3.1–11	1 Pet 5.1–11	1 Cor 15.50–58	1 Pet 1.13–25
Mt 12.38–42	Jn 10.7–18	Lk 24.36–43	Jn 21.1–14

3rd Sunday after Easter

Neh 2.1–18	Lev 19.9–18	Exod 16.4–15	Isa 62.1–5
1 Cor 12.3–13	1 Jn 4.13–21	1 Cor 8.1–13	Rev 3.14–22
Jn 11.17–27	Jn 13.31–35	Jn 6.35–40	Jn 21.15–25

4th Sunday after Easter

2 Sam 1.17–27	Exod 19.1–6	Deut 7.6–11	Ezek 36.24–28
1 John 2.1–11	1 Pet 2.1–10	Gal 3.23–4.7	Gal 5.13–25
Jn 14.1–11	Jn 15.1–11	Jn 15.12–17	Jn 15.18–27

5th Sunday after Easter

1 Kings 18.20–39	Gen 18.23–33	Dan 6.10–23	Exod 33.7–11
Heb 7.11–25, (26–28)	Rom 8.22–27	2 Thess 3.1–5	Rom 8.28–39
Mt 6.1–15	Jn 16.12–24	Lk 7.1–10	Jn 16.25–33

Ascension Day

Dan 7.13–14	Dan 7.13–14	Dan 7.13–14	Dan 7.13–14
Acts 1.1–11	Acts 1.1–11	Acts 1.1–11	Acts 1.1–11
Mt 28.16–20	Mk 16.15–20 or Mk 8.31–9.1	Lk 24.44–53	Jn 16.1–11

Year A	Year B	Year C	Year D

6th Sunday after Easter: Sunday after Ascension

Jer 10.1–10a	Isa 45.1–7	Ezek 43.1–7a	2 Kings 2.1–15
Eph 4.1–16	Eph 1.15–23	Acts 1.12–26	Rev 5.6–14
Lk 24.44–53	Jn 17.1–13	Mt 28.16–20	Jn 7.32–39

Pentecost

Joel 2.23–29	Josh 1.1–9	Gen 11.1–9	Ezek 37.1–14
Acts 2.1–11	Acts 2.1–11	Acts 2.1–11	Acts 2.1–11
Mt 12.14–21	Mk 4.26–34	Lk 11.1–13	Jn 14.15–27
	or		
	Mk 3.19b–30		

1st Sunday after Pentecost: Trinity Sunday

Isa 6.1–8	Deut 6.4–9	Exod 19.3–8, 16–20	Isa 40.12–17
Eph 1.3–14	Rom 8.12–17	Acts 2.(14–21) 22–36	1 Tim 6.11–16
Mt 11.25–30	Mk 1.9–11	Lk 10.17–24	Jn 14.8–17

2nd Sunday after Pentecost

Ezek 18.25–32	2 Chr 15.1–8	2 Sam 7.4–16	Deut 6.17–25
Acts 17.22–34	Acts 4.13–31	Acts 2.37–47	Rom 10.5–17
Mt 3.1–6	Mk 1.29–39	Lk 14.15–24	Jn 3.1–15

3rd Sunday after Pentecost

Isa 60.19–22	1 Sam 16.14–23	Deut 8.11–20	Hab 2.1–4
Phil 2.12–18	Acts 16.16–24	Acts 4.5–12	1 Jn 2.22–29
Mt 5.13–16	Mk 5.1–20	Lk 8.40–56	Jn 3.22–36

4th Sunday after Pentecost

Deut 26.1–11	Amos 7.10–15	Ezek 34.1–6	Micah 4.1–7
2 Cor 8.1–15	Acts 13.1–12	Acts 8.26–38	Heb 12.18–29
Mt 5.21–37	Mk 6.1–13	Lk 15.1–10	Jn 4.5–26

Year A	Year B	Year C	Year D

5th Sunday after Pentecost

Year A	Year B	Year C	Year D
Isa 49.14–21	Esth 4.10–5.8	Ruth 1.1–18 (19–22)	Jonah (3.6–10) 4.1–11
Acts 4.32–37	Acts 13.13–25	Acts 11.4–18	Eph 2.11–22
Mt 6.22–34	Mk 6.14–29	Lk 17.11–19	Jn 4.27–42

6th Sunday after Pentecost

Year A	Year B	Year C	Year D
2 Chr 6.12–21	Jer 23.23–32	Jer 38.1–13	Hos 14.1–7
1 Tim 2.1–8	Gal 5.2–11	Acts 20.7–12	Acts 9.36–43
Mt 7.1–14	Mk 8.14–21	Lk 7.11–17	Jn 4.43–54

7th Sunday after Pentecost

Year A	Year B	Year C	Year D
Jer 7.1–7	1 Kings 10.1–13	1 Sam 24.7b–17	Micah 7.14–20
Acts 19.13–20	1 Tim 3.14–16	Gal 6.1–10	Acts 24.10–21
Mt 7.15–29	Mk 8.22–26	Lk 7.36–50	Jn 5.19–36

8th Sunday after Pentecost

Year A	Year B	Year C	Year D
Gen 21.(1–8) 9–21	1 Sam 17.(32–37) 38–50	Josh 2.1–14	Isa 43.1–13
Rom 9.19–28	2 Cor 6.1–10	Phil 4.1–3	Acts 27.33–44
Mt 8.5–13	Mk 9.14–29	Lk 8.1–3	Jn 6.16–21

9th Sunday after Pentecost

Year A	Year B	Year C	Year D
Hos 6.1–6	Num 11.24–29	1 Kings 19.(1–8) 9–21	1 Kings 17.8–16
2 Cor 5.14–6.2	1 Cor 12.14–26	1 Pet 3.13–22	Rom 14.10–23
Mt 9.9–13	Mk 9.33–41	Lk 9.51–62	Jn 6.22–27

10th Sunday after Pentecost

Year A	Year B	Year C	Year D
Jonah 3.1–5	Deut 10.12–11.1	Exod 22.21–27	Prov 9.9–11
Acts 9.26–31	Heb 12.3–13	Rom 12.9–21	1 Cor 11.23–29
Mt 9.35–10.16	Mk 9.42–50	Lk 10.25–42	Jn 6.41–59

Year A	Year B	Year C	Year D
11th Sunday after Pentecost			
Jer 20.7–13	Isa 54.1–8	Ezek 12.21–28	Judg 6.36–40
Acts 20.17–35	Eph 5.21–6.4	1 Thess 1.1–10	1 Jn 5.1–5
Mt 10.16–25	Mk 10.13–16	Lk 12.35–48	Jn 7.1–17
12th Sunday after Pentecost			
Gen 24.62–67	Mic 6.1–8	Amos 5.18–24	Job 28.12–28
Col 3.18–4.1	Eph 4.17–32	Jas 1.19–27	1 Cor 2.11–3.9
Mt 12.43–50	Mk 10.46–52	Lk 13.(1–9) 10–17	Jn 7.40–52
13th Sunday after Pentecost			
Hab 3.17–19	Isa 5.1–7	Exod 23.10–13	Exod 34.4–9
Rom 8.18–25	Acts 13.44–52	Rom 14.1–9	Rom 7.1–6
Mt 13.24–43	Mk 12.1–12	Lk 14.1–6	Jn 8.3–11
14th Sunday after Pentecost			
1 Kings 3.4–15	Hos 11.1–9	Prov 25.2–7	Exod 13.17–22
1 Cor 15.35–52	1 Cor 12.27–13.13	2 Cor 11.7–15	Eph 5.11–20
Mt 13.44–52	Mk 12.28–34	Lk 14.7–14	Jn 8.12–20
15th Sunday after Pentecost			
Ezek 37.15a–28	1 Kings 21.1–16	2 Sam 18.(24–30) 31–33	Jer 28.1–17
1 Cor 1.10–17	Gal 1.1–10	Gal 6.14–18	1 Jn 5.10–21
Mt 18.10–20	Mk 12.35–44	Lk 14.25–35	Jn 8.(31–36) 37–47
16th Sunday after Pentecost			
Gen 45.1–15	Deut 15.1–11	Gen 37.(2–11) 12–28	Jer 50.4–7
Jas 2.8–13	2 Cor 9.6–15	Col 3.12–17	1 Pet 2.11–25
Mt 18.21–35	Mk 14.1–9	Lk 15.11–32	Jn 10.1–6

Year A	Year B	Year C	Year D
17th Sunday after Pentecost			
Exod 20.1–17	Exod 12.21–27	Amos 8.4–7	2 Chr 7.11–16
Eph 5.1–5	Heb 9.23–28	1 Tim 6.1–12	Eph 3.14–21
Mt 19.13–30	Mk 14.10–25	Lk 16.1–13	Jn 10.22–30
18th Sunday after Pentecost			
Eccles 3.1–13	Gen 32.22–32	Amos 6.1–7	Prov 3.13–20
2 Thess 3.6–13	Col 1.21–29	Jas 2.1–9	Rom 11.33–36
Mt 20.1–16	Mk 14.26–42	Lk 16.19–31	Jn 10.31–42
19th Sunday after Pentecost			
Josh 6.1–20	Exod 32.7–14	Lev 25.39–46	Dan 12.1–4
Heb 11.17–22, 29–31	Heb 6.4–9	Philem 1–25	2 Cor 5.1–10
Mt 21.18–32	Mk 14.43–52	Lk 17.1–10	Jn 11.1–16
20th Sunday after Pentecost			
Deut 4.1–8	Dan 3.13–26	Gen 6.5–8	Job 42.1–6
Rom 13.1–10	Acts 5.27–42	Phil 1.1–11	Phil 1.12–30
Mt 22.15–22	Mk 14.53–65	Lk 17.20–37	Jn 11.28–44
21st Sunday after Pentecost			
Neh 6.1–16	Exod 2.11–22	Gen 17.1–10	Judg 11.29–40
1 Pet 4.7–11	Heb 11.23–28	Rom 4.1–12	Heb 9.11–15 (16–22)
Mt 25.14–30	Mk 14.66–72	Lk 19.1–10	Jn 11.45–54
22nd Sunday after Pentecost			
Isa 45.14–25	2 Sam 16.1–13	Num 27.15–23	2 Sam 23.13–17
Acts 15.1–2, 22–29	Acts 7.54–8.1	Acts 8.5–8, 14–17	Acts 6.1–7
Mt 26.6–13	Mk 15.1–21	Lk 20.1–8	Jn 13.12–30

Year A	Year B	Year C	Year D

Last Sunday after Pentecost

Year A	Year B	Year C	Year D
Isa 33.17–22	Isa 25.1–9	Judg 7.1–8, 19–23	Jer 29.1, 4–14
Rev 7.9–17	Rev 7. 2–4, 9–12	Heb 11.32–12.2	Phil 3.7–21
Mt 25.1–13	Mt 5.1–12	Lk 19.11–27	Jn 17.13–26

Harvest Festival

Year A	Year B	Year C	Year D
Gen 8.15–22	Lev 25.15–22	Gen 41.1–7, 25–32	Deut 26.1–11 or Lev 19.9–18
Gal 6.7–10	Phil 4.10–20	Rev 14.14–18	2 Cor 9.6–15
Mt 6.25–34	Mk 4.1–9, 13–20	Lk 12.16–31	Jn 12.23–28

Acknowledgements

List of Abbreviations and Publication Details

ASB   Alphabetic Sayings Bible (Q text)
CPW   Contemporary Prayers for Public Worship
GNB   Good News Bible
JB   Jerusalem Bible
NEB   New English Bible
NIV   New International Version
REB   Revised English Bible
RSV   Revised Standard Version

RESOURCES FOR PUBLICATION

Acknowledgements

List of Abbreviations used in Acknowledgements.

ASB   Alternative Service Book, 1980.
CPPW   Contemporary Prayers For Public Worship.
GNB   Good News Bible.
JB   Jerusalem Bible.
NEB   New English Bible.
NIV   New International Version.
REB   Revised English Bible.
RSV   Revised Standard Version.

RESOURCES FOR PUBLIC WORSHIP

Calls to Worship and Scripture Sentences: 'We have come together . . .' and 'The Lord is here; . . .' from *The Alternative Service Book 1980* © The Central Board of Finance of the Church of England: Lamentations 3:22–23, John 1:14, 2 Corinthians 4:5, 6 from the *Revised English Bible* © 1989 by permission of Oxford and Cambridge University Presses: Psalm 100:4–5 from *The Psalms* by Harry Mowvley (1989), © Harry Mowvley, by permission of Collins Publishers: Psalm 89:1–2 and James 4:8a, 10 from the *Jerusalem Bible* (Darton, Longman & Todd).

Invocation: Psalm 19:14 and Jeremiah 14:9 from the *Holy Bible, New International Version*, © 1973, 1978, 1984 by International Bible Society. Used with permission: 'Lord God, we pray . . .' adapted from prayer 1 p. 77 of *Prayers for Use in Church*. Used by permission of The Saint Andrew Press.

Praise and Thanksgiving: 'Lord God, creator of all things, . . .' after John Baillie, *A Diary of Private Prayer*, p. 9 (OUP 1936). Used with permission.

Adoration: Ephesians 3:20–21 from *NIV*: Revelation 5:12–13 from *Revised Standard Version Bible* copyright 1946, 1952, 1971 by the Division of Christian Education of the National Council of the Churches of Christ in the USA. Used by permission: 'Glory to God in the highest, ...' from the English Translation of the *Gloria in Excelsis* prepared by the International Consultation on English Texts and revised in 1990 by the English Language Liturgical Consultation: Psalm 89:8, 11b, 13b, 14, 15a, 52 and 1 Chronicles 29:10b, 11, 13 from *REB*.

Confession: 'Almighty God, our heavenly Father, ...' from *ASB*; 'Merciful God, ...' from *Contemporary Prayers for Public Worship* ed. Caryl Micklem (SCM Press, 1967).

Assurance of Forgiveness: 1 John 1:8–9 from *REB*; 'Listen to him, ...' from *CPPW*.

Prayers Before Reading or Preaching: both from *The Book of Common Order* (Church of Scotland).

Prayers for Ourselves: 'To love someone else's life ...' from *New Prayers for Worship* by Alan Gaunt (John Paul the Preacher's Press, 1972); 'Almighty God, to whom all hearts are open, ...' from *ASB*.

Intercession: 'O God, we commend to your blessing ...' from Jamie Wallace, *There's a Time and a Place* (Collins 1982), © S. J. Wallace.

Offering: 'To you who are our life ...' from *There's a Time and a Place* op. cit.; 'Lord Jesus Christ, ...' from *CPPW*; 'Lord, you judge us not by what we give, ...' previously unpublished. Used by permission of the author, Frank Cooke.

Blessings and Benedictions: Luke 2:29–32 from the English Translation of the *Nunc Dimittis* prepared by the International Consultation on English Texts and revised in 1990 by the English Language Liturgical Consultation; 'Lighten our darkness, Lord, we pray; ...' from *ASB*; 'Be the eye of God ...' from *Carmina Gadelica* ... collected by Alexander Carmichael (Edinburgh: Scottish Academic Press,

6 vols. from 1900), vol. iii ed. Prof. James Carmichael
Watson, p. 205; 'The grace of the Lord Jesus Christ . . .'
translation of 2 Corinthians 13:14 from Frances Young and
David Ford, *Meaning and Truth in 2 Corinthians* (SPCK
1987). Used with permission: Ephesians 3:18, 19 from *New
English Bible*, 2nd edn. © 1970, by permission of Oxford
and Cambridge University Presses; 'The blessing of God
almighty, . . .' from *ASB*.

The Lord's Prayer: 'Our Father in heaven . . .' from *ASB*.

Worship Through the Year:

DISCIPLESHIP: M. J. Walker, 'Lord, remembering the depth of
your love to us, . . .' from *Praise God: a collection of resource
material for Christian worship*, by Alec Gilmore, Edward
Smalley, and Michael Walker (1980). Used with permission of
Mrs A. M. Walker.

FAMILY LIFE: 'God, father and mother of us all, . . .' from
There's a Time and a Place by Jamie Wallace (Collins 1982),
© S. J. Wallace.

THE CROSS: from *Praise God* by Alec Gilmore, Edward
Smalley, and Michael Walker (The Baptist Union of Great
Britain 1980).

RESURRECTION: 'It is fitting . . .', © Fellowship of St Alban
and St Sergius. Used with permission.

EXALTATION: M. J. Walker, 'Forgive us, Father, . . .' from
Praise God by Alec Gilmore, Edward Smalley, and Michael
Walker. Used by permission of Mrs A. M. Walker.

HARVEST; 'God our Father, . . .' from N. Dixon (ed.),
*Companion to the Lectionary, Vol. 3: A New Collection of
Prayers* (Epworth Press, 1983), pp. 192–3. Used with
permission.

REMEMBRANCE SUNDAY: 'The righteous man, . . .' and 'The
righteous live for ever . . .' both from *RSV* op. cit.

THE TWO MINUTES SILENCE: 'They shall grow not old . . .'

from 'For the Fallen (September 1914)'. By permission of Mrs Nicolete Gray and The Society of Authors on behalf of the Laurence Binyon Estate: 'Almighty Father . . .' from N. Dixon (ed.), *Companion to the Lectionary, Vol. 3: A New Collection of Prayers* (Epworth Press, 1983), p. 183. Used by permission.

THE LORD'S SUPPER: The First Pattern

Gospel Words: Psalm 116:12, Isaiah 53:6, 5, John 3:16, Romans 5:8, John 6:51, and Revelation 3:20 from *NEB* op. cit.; Matthew 11:28–29 and Romans 8:15–16 from *NIV* op. cit.

Institution: 1 Corinthians 11:23–26 and Matthew 26:19–22, 26–29 from *NIV* op. cit.

Thanksgiving: Breaking of Bread and Distribution/Sharing the Cup: from *NIV*.

Second Pattern:

Invitation to the Table: 'Come to this table, . . .' after p. 119 of *The Lord's Supper* by W. Barclay (SCM Press, 1967).

Gospel Words: John 6:35 from *NEB*; John 6:51 and 1 Corinthians 10:16–17, both from *REB*; Revelation 3:20 from *Good News Bible*, published by the Bible Societies/Collins, © New Testament: American Bible Society, New York, 1966, 1971, and 4th edn. 1976, reproduced with the permission of the publishers.

Prayer of Preparation or Confession: 'Almighty God, . . .' from *ASB* op. cit.; 'Lord, we come to your table . . .' from *Methodist Service Book*.

The Peace: 'Christ is our peace . . .', 'We are the Body of Christ . . .' and 'The peace of the Lord be always with you . . .' from *ASB* op. cit.

Institution: 1 Corinthians 11:23–26 from *REB* op. cit.

Sharing the Bread: 1 Corinthians 10:16–17 ibid.

The Lifting of the Cup: Psalm 116:12–14, and 1 Corinthians 11:25, ibid.

Prayer or Words of Acclamation: 'Almighty God, we thank you for feeding us . . .' and 'Father of all, we give you thanks . . .' from *ASB* op. cit.; 'Most gracious God, . . .' from *United Reformed Church Service Book* (1989).

THE BAPTISM OF BELIEVERS AND RECEPTION INTO MEMBERSHIP: First Pattern

Introduction: Galatians 3:27 from *REB* op. cit.

The Laying on of Hands: 1 Peter 2:9, Matthew 5:14a, 16, and Ephesians 2:19–20, ibid.

INFANT PRESENTATION: First Pattern

Readings: Matthew 18:3–4 and Mark 10:13–16, from *REB* op. cit

Prayers of Thanksgiving: 'Lord God, we praise you, . . .' from *REB* op. cit.

Blessing: Numbers 6:24–26 from *REB*; Numbers 6:24–26 from *RSV* op. cit.

Second Pattern:

Prayer of Thanksgiving: 'God our Father, . . .' from *ASB* op. cit.

Prayer for the Family's Future: ibid.

CHRISTIAN MARRIAGE

Call to worship: 'Living God, you have commanded us to love each other. . .' from *New Prayers for Worship* by Alan Gaunt (John Paul the Preacher's Press, 1972).

Declaration of Purpose: after *The Alternative Service Book 1980* p. 288 op. cit.

The Giving of the Rings: ibid.

Declaration of Marriage: from *Praise God* by Alec Gilmore, Edward Smalley and Michael Walker (The Baptist Union of Great Britain 1980).

Prayer and Blessing: Numbers 6:24–26 from *RSV*.

Additional material: '—I will love you in good times and bad . . .' from *New Prayers for Worship* op. cit. 'Lord God, Heavenly Father, . . .' from *A Christian Celebration of Marriage*, The Consultation on Common Texts (Fortress Press), copyright 1987 Hans C. Boehringer. All rights reserved.

THE FUNERAL: First Pattern

Sentences: Lamentations 3:22–23 from *ASB* op. cit.; Matthew 5:4 from *RSV*; Isaiah 66:13 from *United Reformed Church Service Book* (1989); 1 Peter 1:3–4 from *NEB* op. cit.; Romans 8:38–39 from *REB* op. cit. 'Eternal God, the Lord of life, . . .' from *Methodist Service Book*.

The Act of Committal: 1 Corinthians 15:55, 57 and Revelation 21:4 from *REB*; 'Now, Lord, let your servant go in peace: . . .' from *ASB* op. cit.; 'God of peace, . . .' from *CPPW* p. 108, op. cit.

A Service of Thanksgiving:

Assurance of Forgiveness: 'Here is a saying you must trust, . . .' from *REB* op. cit.

THE FUNERAL: Second Pattern

Sentences: John 11:25–26 from *GNB* op. cit.; Deuteronomy 33:27 from *NIV*; John 3:16 and John 5:25 from *RSV*; 1 Corinthians 2:9 from *REB* op. cit.

Welcome: 'We are here to honour . . .' from *Praise God* op. cit.; 'Father, your love is stronger than death: . . .' after *CPPW* p. 105 op. cit.

Thanksgiving for Victory over death: 'Lord God, with your whole Church . . .' from *CPPW* p. 105; 'Living God, we praise you . . .' from *Praise God* op. cit.

For those who mourn: 'Almighty God, Father of all mercies . . .' from *The Alternative Service Book 1980*; 'O God of infinite compassion, . . .' from *Methodist Service Book*; 'Depart, O Christian soul, . . .' from *Praise God* op. cit.; 1 Peter 5:10–11 from *GNB* op. cit.

The Committal:

Sentences: Revelation 1:17–18, 1 Timothy 6:7 and Job 1:21 from *REB* op. cit.

Prayers and Reflections: 'You, Christ, are the king of glory . . .' from *United Reformed Church Service Book* (1989).

Ascription of Glory and/or Blessing: Jude 24–25 from *GNB* op. cit.; Romans 15:13 from *RSV*.

For the Burial or Scattering of Ashes: Psalm 145:13–14, 10–12, 18, 21 from *NIV* op. cit.; 'We remember — with gratitude . . .' from *United Reformed Church Service Book* (1989).

For a Still-Born or Newly Born Child: Lamentations 3:22–33 from *NEB*; Psalm 55:22 from *RSV*; Hebrews 13:5 from *GNB*; Revelation 7:17 from the *Jerusalem Bible* op. cit.

On the Death of a Child: Isaiah 40:10–11 from *Good News Bible*; Matthew 18:10, 14 from *NEB*.

For a Sudden or Violent Death:

Sentences: Romans 5:8 from *REB* op. cit.

After a Suicide

Sentences: Isaiah 40:3, 4 from *RSV*; 'Lord, you have

examined me . . .'; John 14:18, 27 from *REB* op. cit. Psalm 139:1–3, 23 from *NEB* op. cit. John 14:18, 27 from *Revised English Bible*.

MINISTRY

First Pattern of Ordination: based on the order of service for ordination, Regent's Park College, Oxford. Used with permission.

Second Pattern of Ordination: Laying on of Hands and Ordination Prayer based on a form of ordination material supplied by Spurgeon's College, London.

PROMISES FOR AN ACT OF COMMISSIONING: 2 Timothy 4:4–5, and Ephesians 4:11–13 from *NIV* op. cit.

THE LIFE OF THE CHURCH

Act of Covenanting: John 13:34–35 and Ephesians 2:19–21a from *NEB* op. cit.

Laying a Foundation Stone: Psalm 127:1 and 1 Corinthians 3:11 from *NEB*.

Opening a New Church Building: Psalm 24:7 and Psalm 100:4–5a from *NEB*.

A Service of Healing:

Scripture Sentences: Philippians 4:5b, 6–7 from *NIV* op. cit.; Psalm 145:3, Psalm 37:7 from *RSV*; Matthew 18:20 and Matthew 11:28 from *REB* op. cit.

The Laying on of Hands: Mark 5:34 from *RSV*.

Intercessions: 'Set free, O Lord, . . .' and 'Father, we abandon ourselves . . .' from *The Ministry of Healing in the Church*, © 1963 United Reformed Church, 86 Tavistock Place, London WC1H 9RT. Used with permission.